The Simple Fool's Handbook To Cooking

The
Simple
Fool's
Handbook
To Cooking

A MANUAL FOR THE
COLLEGE-BOUND GOURMAND

**WRITTEN AND CONCEIVED BY
CLIFF MacGILLIVRAY**

ILLUSTRATIONS BY JOHN TORMEY

AVON
PUBLISHERS OF BARD, CAMELOT, DISCUS AND FLARE BOOKS

AVON BOOKS
A division of
The Hearst Corporation
959 Eighth Avenue
New York, New York 10019

First Avon Printing, September, 1981

AVON TRADEMARK REG. U.S. PAT. OFF. AND
IN OTHER COUNTRIES, MARCA REGISTRADA,
HECHO EN U.S.A.

Printed in the U.S.A.

10 9 8 7 6 5 4 3 2 1

To Mom and Dad — who were forced to eat the great things in this book and the not so great things that aren't.

Contents

Introduction

As Harold awoke from his slumber in the summer sun, he could smell the scrumptious, roasting turkey twenty feet away. He could close his eyes and taste the tender, moist slices of the freshly-cooked bird. He could hear the gurgling, bubbling, churning creek as it wound to and fro and here and there gliding through the green, plush countryside to the soft, quiet, shaded pools below. Harold lay there by the pools and let the smells and sounds of freshness caress him.

"Harold," his roomate nagged, "quit daydreaming, get off your butt, come over here and eat your beans before they get cold." Harold was shaken back into reality. "College students shouldn't have to eat beans every night," he thought. "There must be some way I can learn how to cook something else. Perhaps I could buy one of those fancy cookbooks with those exciting titles like, 'Tasty Meatloaf Dish' or '300 Ways To Make Hamburger Taste Better'. But all those books have lists of ingredients I've never even heard of, let alone want to eat; ingredients like zunge, anchovy paste, and fegato. I don't want to eat spaghetti, hot dogs, and peanut butter the rest of my life! I also know that next to eating out, the most expensive thing I can do is rely on convenience foods. I'm no dummy. On a student budget, I can't afford an expensive diet. But my stomach can't afford much more of this punishment."

Well this book is just what Harold and everyone else like him needs. It has over 150 tasty, economy-minded, quick'n'easy recipes. It has simple directions any idiot can follow with results anyone will be happy with. . .

In the six chapters that follow, I have tried to cover most areas of cooking important to the simple, inexperienced fool learning how to cook. Main dishes, meats, vegetables, and salads all have their very own chapters. There is also a chapter on how to survive on dorm cooking for those of you unfortunate enough to be trapped in a dorm room with no cooking facilities. Finally, there's some helpful hints and a few miscellaneous items that will help you master the culinary arts. This book is written by a college student for college students and other types who have been thrown out on their own and don't know the first thing about cooking.

I would like to say a couple of things regarding my recipes. First of all, since I did write this for the college student, I've assumed that you're a fairly intelligent bunch. Therefore, I have no doubts that you will be able to figure out things like "salt to taste" or what amounts to prepare depending on the number of people you are serving or how hungry you are. Secondly, there are probably some ingredients in some of these dishes you don't like, things like bell peppers or onions or whatever. If you don't like them they can usually be left out but you'll be missing out on the flavor they add. Plus, someday you're going to grow up, become a prominent doctor, lawyer, or surgical tubing salesman and you'll be at a big dinner party and you won't be able to pick out your onions or green peppers. You'll have to eat them then, so you might as well go ahead and give them a try now.

Cliff MacGillivray

The Simple Fool's Handbook To Cooking

Thirty Meals

Thirty Meals

As you might have guessed, this chapter has one good meal for every day of the month, except of course, for February when you're forced to skip two. Or perhaps any month with thirty-one days when you get to eat your favorite twice. In any event, there are thirty tasty meals in here that should keep your little tummy from grumbling. Most of them are meals in themselves, but occasionally you might have to serve them with vegetables or potatoes or whatever (then you can turn to Chapter 3). They are good recipes that don't call for too many spices. I don't see any reason to buy a can of "minty forest mushroom flakes" if you're only going to use them in one recipe. Some of the recipes call for oregano, parsley flakes, paprika, or other often-used spices, but nothing too wild. However, you will find the more you cook the more you will experiment and the more flavor-enhancing spices can be. But this I will let you discover by yourself.

There is no great need for cooking equipment, either. If you have a stove, a couple of casserole dishes (one- and two-quart sizes), a frying pan, and a baking dish, you're just about set.

About half of these recipes are for three or four normal people or two lumberjack types. If you don't have three or four normal people, you can always cut the recipe in half, invite somebody over for dinner, or reheat the leftovers in aluminum foil. In other words, you'll just have to use your head (figuratively speaking — not in the recipe). The remainder of the meals are very flexible; you can prepare enough to serve one to a hundred, depending on how hungry they are. So here they are, thirty of the quickest, easiest, best meals you'll ever eat.

BEEF OLE is a great Spanish style dish. The corn chips make it nice and crunchy. If you eat it once, you'll eat it again.

BEEF OLE

1 lb. ground round	1 tsp. oregano
1 chopped onion	1 tsp. garlic powder
1 chopped bell pepper	salt, pepper to taste
1 6 oz. can of tomato paste	tomatoes sliced and quartered
1 cup water	shredded lettuce
1 package corn chips	grated cheddar cheese
½ tsp. paprika	

Brown the meat and onion, add the bell pepper, tomato paste, water, and spices. Bring to a boil and cover, simmer for 25 minutes. Prepare tomatoes, cheese, and lettuce, keeping in separate bowls. When the meat sauce is done, spread some corn chips on a plate, pour the meat sauce over them, and add the cheese, tomato, and lettuce toppings. Have everybody serve themselves.

This is just a super sparerib recipe with a sweet and sour sauce. The only way to describe it is. . .

DELICIOUS SPARERIBS

2 to 3 lbs. country style spareribs	1 cup brown sugar
5 apples	6 or 8 whole cloves

Place the ribs in a casserole dish. Slice the apples and lay them over the ribs. Sprinkle brown sugar and cloves on top. Bake at 325 for 1½ to 2 hours until ribs are tender. Serve over piping hot rice.

If you're a mushroom fan, you'll love this one—even if you're not a mushroom fan, you'll still enjoy it.

MUSHROOM CASSEROLE

1 lb. fresh mushrooms
1 can undiluted mushroom soup
8 slices white bread
1½ cups milk
2 eggs
½ cup chopped onion

½ cup chopped celery
½ cup bell pepper
½ cup mayonnaise
salt, pepper to taste
grated cheddar cheese

Slice the mushrooms and saute them. Add onion, celery, bell peppers, and mayonnaise. Set aside. Butter and cube three slices of bread and place them in the bottom of a casserole dish. Pour the mushroom mix on top. Add three more slices of buttered, cubed bread. Beat the eggs, mixing them with the milk and pour on top. Place in the refrigerator for one hour. Add the can of soup and the last two slices of bread. Bake at 325 for 50 minutes. Sprinkle some grated cheddar cheese on top and bake for 10 more minutes.

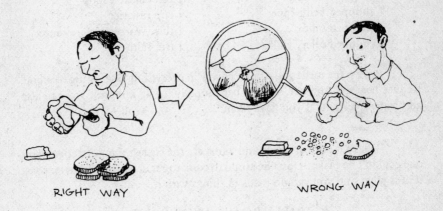

RIGHT WAY   WRONG WAY

Note: It is easier to butter the bread before cubing it.

This is probably the best recipe in the book. It's one of the recipes to which you can add varied amounts of the ingredients and it will still taste good. The beansprouts are a must, they make it nice and crunchy. Don't skip them or it won't be the same.

VEGEDILLAS

Roll up the following ingredients in a large flour tortilla:

handful of beansprouts   freshly sliced mushrooms
grated Monterey jack cheese   chopped tomatoes
grated cheddar cheese

Use a toothpick to hold them together, then pan fry them in butter on a medium flame until they start to get crisp and brown. Some other additions you can make are wheat germ, nuts, hot sauce, peppers, or just use your imagination.

This is a good meal with a distinct oriental flavor.

ASIAN MIX

1 lb. ground round   1 can chicken soup
1 chopped bell pepper   1 cup raw rice
1 chopped onion   1 tbls. Worcestershire sauce
2 chopped celery stalks   1 tsp. salt

Brown the meat and drain. Throw in everything else. Bring to a boil. Reduce heat and simmer, stirring occasionally for 45 minutes. You can also add water chestnuts if you have them.

Believe it or not, roasts and hams are the easiest things to cook. This one couldn't be easier. Don't be afraid to cook too much meat. Leftover roast beef is great and you can do loads of things with it.

SIMPLE ROAST AND GRAVY

Wrap one 4 to 5 pound rump roast or eye of round in aluminum foil. Leave a 1″ x 3″ slit on top so the roast will brown. Bake at 325 for 4 hours until it's moist and tender.

THE GRAVY

Pour roast juice in frying pan, thickening with quick-mixing enriched flour. Shake flour slowly and stir until desired thickness is reached. (You can add water to thin.) Bring to a boil. Serve over mashed potatoes. (Chapter 3)

OK, I said you can use leftover roast beef for almost anything. Here's my favorite recipe; there's more in Chapter 2.

LEFTOVER ROAST CASSEROLE

2 cups cubed roast beef
1 small onion chopped finely
4 sliced carrots

2 cups Bisquick mix
1 tin of mushroom gravy
leftover gravy, if available

Throw everything but the Bisquick mix into a casserole dish. In a separate dish, combine 2 cups Bisquick mix and 1 cup cold water. Drop by spoonfuls on top of meat and vegetable mix. Bake at 400 until crust is done. (About 20 minutes.)

This is a classic fish recipe. You can use almost any kind of fish. It calls for frozen halibut boneless filets, although trout and salmon are just as good.

EASIEST FISH RECIPE IN THE WORLD

frozen halibut boneless filets

Just melt a hunk of butter over medium heat. Fry the fish (still frozen) 5 minutes on each side. That's all there is to it. If you don't like it with a little lemon, try the seafood sauce in Chapter 6.

Here's a meal that tastes sort of like a taco in a casserole dish. It's really good.

CRISPY MEXICAN CASSEROLE (No, it doesn't have Mexicans in it.)

1 lb. ground round
1 chopped onion
1 garlic clove minced
1 can tomato sauce
$^1/_3$ can water
1 can kidney beans

¼ tsp. oregano
2 tbls. chili powder
1 bag corn chips
lettuce
cheddar cheese
more onion

Brown the meat, onion, and garlic. Add in the tomato sauce, water, oregano, and chili powder. In a large casserole dish, alternate layers of this mixture with beans and corn chips, finishing with corn chips on top. Bake covered at 350 for 45 minutes. Uncover, shred some cheese, lettuce, and onions on top. Bake for 10 minutes and serve.

This recipe is considerably cheaper than going to your local chicken place, much healthier, and you know what you're eating. I'm not knocking those fast food chains but I have a friend whose sister worked in one of the leading chicken places and after three months she became a vegetarian. I don't know about you but that tells me something—I'd rather eat my chicken at home.

SUPER EASY SUPER FAST CHICKEN

1 cut up chicken

Place chicken on a cookie sheet covered with aluminum foil, skin side up. Butter generously, salt lightly. Bake at 325 for 1 hour. You can put some medium sized potatoes in at the same time. Make a salad and you're set.

Nothing like a hard day's ridin' and ropin' to get you good and hungry. You brand that new calf and now as the sun sinks down, you need something to really stick to your ribs. You saunter on over to the chuck wagon where Zeb has done it again, (for the 107th night in a row). He serves you. . .

GOOD OLD FASHIONED CHILI

1 lb. ground round	1 chopped onion
2 cans kidney beans	1 tbls. chili powder
1 can tomato soup	1 tsp. salt

Brown meat, drain. Throw in everything else, mix well, and bring to a boil. Reduce heat and simmer for at least 40 minutes (the longer, the better) stirring occasionally.

I am sure you are already aware there are a million different recipes for chili, spaghetti, and other popular meals. They have world champion chili contests where people add everything you can imagine to their chili, even beer (which come to think of it, was probably one of the first imagined). There are also packet meals in your local food store that have recipes for most popular meals, and all you have to do is buy them and follow the directions on the package. But why buy packaged meals when you can whip up your own? I admit my recipes are not quite as easy to prepare, but they are cheaper in the long run and much tastier. In any event, here's a simple, easy, tasty spaghetti recipe.

MEATY SPAGHETTI SAUCE

1 lb. ground round
½ cup chopped onions
½ cup chopped bell peppers
2 cups thinly sliced mushrooms
1 8 oz. can tomato sauce

¼ tsp. oregano
1 tsp. garlic powder
1 sprinkle of parsley flakes
salt, pepper to taste.

Brown the meat, drain. Add everything else, mix well, and bring to a boil, reduce heat and simmer 20 minutes. Serve over hot noodles with parmesan cheese.

One of my old roommates used to come up with quite a few surprises out of our kitchen. (We were surprised anyone could eat them.) One of the group favorites was this tasty burger dish. It's good with rice because it has lots of sauce.

STUFFED BURGER BUNDLES

1 lb. ground beef
1½ cups stuffing
1 can cream of mushroom soup

⅓ cup evaporated milk
1 tbls. ketchup
2 tsp. Worcestershire sauce

Prepare stuffing, combine meat with evaporated milk, dividing into 5 patties. Pat each patty into a 6 inch circle. Put ¼ cup stuffing in center of each one. Close meat around stuffing. Place in casserole dish. Combine remaining ingredients and pour over meat. Bake, uncovered at 350 for 35 to 40 minutes.

This recipe is one of the great cheapies, usually running about 30¢ per person

TUNA MACARONI CASSEROLE

2 cans macaroni and cheese
2 cans tuna

grated cheddar cheese

Alternate layers of macaroni and tuna in a greased casserole dish. Sprinkle the cheese on top and bake uncovered at 300 for 30 minutes.

Tacos are the most popular Mexican food in the United States. In Mexico, the word taco simply means "snack," and there are many variations of the ingredients, toppings, and tortillas. Here in the U.S., taco basically refers to a corn tortilla, folded in half with a hearty meat sauce, tomato, lettuce, and cheese topping. With this in mind, here is an excellent American taco recipe.

YOUR BASIC AMERICAN TACO

corn tortillas
1 lb. ground round
½ cup chopped onion
1 tsp. garlic salt
1 tsp. chili powder

½ tsp. oregano
salt, pepper to taste
finely chopped tomatoes
shredded lettuce
grated cheddar cheese

Tortillas: Heat about 1 inch of oil in a frying pan until a drop of water spits at you. Drop tortillas one at a time into oil. Using 2 forks, fold tortilla into a U shape. Hold tortilla folded until it keeps its shape and is slightly browned and crisp. Drain on paper towels.

Meat Sauce: Brown crumbled meat and onion. Add chili powder, oregano, salt, pepper, and garlic salt. Simmer until cooked. Fill each tortilla with meat sauce. Top with lettuce, cheese, and tomatoes. Add hot sauce if you like.

This next recipe is a good pork and beans dish that tastes a lot better than just plain canned stuff.

PORK AND BEANS

1 lb. can of pork and beans
½ cup chopped onions
½ cup chopped celery
1 lb. hot dogs

2 large tomatoes
½ cup grated cheese
1 tsp. garlic salt

Saute onion and celery. Mix in pork and beans, sliced tomatoes, and garlic. Pour this mix into a greased casserole dish. Lay the hot dogs on top and bake uncovered at 350 for 40 minutes. Grate some cheese on top and continue baking until it melts.

CORNFLAKE CASSEROLE

I know when you first glanced at the name "Cornflake Casserole," you probably turned up your nose and went "ooo-blah." Well, it tastes a lot better than it sounds. (You can just be thankful that I left "Prune Delight" out of the book.)

1 lb. ground beef	1 can tomato soup
1 chopped onion	¼ cup water
1 pkg. cornflakes (regular size)	grated cheddar cheese

Brown meat and onion. Mix with noodles, tomato soup, and water. Pour in a greased casserole dish. Place a thin layer of cornflakes on top, grate some cheese over that, and bake at 350 for 1 hour.

This is an easy-to-prepare ham dinner that Mom always made and the family always loved. (Note: Even when you get a ham that says "pre-cooked," it's good to cook it a little yourself. . .you just can't believe everything you read.)

HAM DINNER

1 pre-cooked ham	baking potatoes
1 bell squash	

Select a nice pre-cooked ham, wrap it in aluminum foil. Slice squash in quarters and clean out the seeds. Butter, and poke little holes in it to let the steam escape. Add scrubbed potatoes and bake everything at 350 for 1½ hours.

This is an excellent, different way to prepare steak. The sauce has an authentic Japanese taste, not like that powdered instant stuff.

TERIYAKI STEAK

2 lbs. steak	1 cup rice

KOICHI'S TERIYAKI SAUCE

½ cup soy sauce	pinch garlic
½ cup sugar	pinch ginger
¼ cup water	1 tsp. butter

Cut the steak while it's still frozen, cutting it as thin as you can into 3 or 4 inch strips. Marinate the steak for ½ hour in the teriyaki sauce. If you're going to marinate it longer for some reason, add ¼ cup of water per ½ hour extra. Fry the thin strips on a medium high flame in a small amount of butter and the sauce. Serve over the piping hot rice.

Here's a college student staple, one of the most inexpensive meals around.

MACARONI AND CHEESE

1 8 oz. elbow macaroni	2 tbls. butter
¼ ½ lb. grated cheese	¼ cup milk

Follow the directions on the package for cooking the macaroni, drain, add everything else. Mix well and bake at 350 for 20 minutes.

I probably could have saved a lot of lives if I'd gotten this book out sooner. Legend has it that all those people jumping off the Golden Gate Bridge were doing so because they couldn't find this recipe. So, in the interest of saving mankind, here's the great San Francisco recipe.

FOR THE LOVE OF A BURGER!

GOLDEN GATER

1 lb. ground round	2 eggs
1 pkg. frozen spinach	salt, pepper to taste
½ cup chopped onion	

Brown the meat and onion in oil. Add the spinach and stir until heated throughout. Add the eggs, salt, and stir until cooked. (Actually, I just made that story up about the Golden Gate to get you to try this recipe.)

This recipe here is a sort of Oriental-Spanish-Americanized-Italian-tasting dish. But relax, the directions are in English.

SPANISH CASSEROLE DISH

1 lb. ground round	2 cans tomato sauce
1 large chopped onion	grated cheddar cheese
1 pkg. narrow noodles	salt, pepper to taste

Boil the noodles 10 minutes and drain. Brown the meat and onion, salt and pepper to taste. Place half the noodles in the bottom of a greased casserole dish. Pour over this, one half of the meat. 1 can of tomato sauce and some grated cheese. Add the remaining meat, sauce, cheese in a 2nd layer. Bake at 300 for 20 minutes.

This is one of those recipes that serves from one to one hundred, depending on how many people you have and how hungry they are. I have added 2 marinating sauces because I couldn't choose a favorite. This is a great dish for entertaining because it tastes like it took a lot of work but didn't.

STEAK KABOB

1 lb. 1″ beef cubes	canned whole small onions
green pepper strips	cherry tomatoes
fresh mushrooms	

MARY'S SPECIAL SAUCE

⅓ cup Worcestershire sauce	1 tbls. water
⅔ cup vinegar	parsley flakes

SAUCE #2

¼ cup red wine
¼ cup olive oil
1 garlic clove

pinch of oregano
pinch of thyme

Cut up the beef into 1 inch cubes. Place on a barbecue skewer alternating with other ingredients. Marinate in a pan for ½ hour in one of the above sauces, and broil.

Here's dish that's exciting, vivacious, stimulating, delightful, enchanting, charming, palatable, savory, enrapturing, and fulfilling. When you eat it you will bubble in sheer ecstasy. The taste will inflame you into a delirious frenzy of red heat. You will be titillated beyond all realms of pleasure. Your tastebuds will tingle, twitter, and then run amok when you bite into this incredibly satisfying meat loaf. Yes, meat loaf. Well, I tried, but no matter what you say about it, it's still meat loaf. However, this is one of the best recipes around. I know that "meat loaf" is a turn-off for a lot of people, but this stuff speaks for itself. It's actually quite good, in fact it's a totally consuming, stroking of the palate; it gives you new meaning to life; it's. . .

EXCITING MEAT LOAF

2 lbs. ground beef
2 eggs
½ cup chopped onion
½ cup chopped green pepper
½ cup chopped celery
2½ cups milk

½ tsp. paprika
salt, pepper to taste
1 cup croutons or crumbled bread
1½ cups grated cheese (cheddar, Monterey Jack, or swiss)

Throw everything together, mixing well. Put in a greased pan and bake uncovered for 1½ hours at 350.

The burrito is like the American hamburger—you can put anything in it. In fact, I understand the burrito is just like a snack down there, and you just toss anything that's not nailed down or red hot (or barking) right into it.

BURRITOS

ground round	diced green chiles
refried beans	chopped red pepper
chopped onions	sliced mushrooms
hot sauce	chopped bell pepper
grated Monterey jack cheese	chopped tomato

What I usually do is brown the meat and drain it. Add the beans, whatever other ingredients you want, and heat the whole thing up. Then I slop this mix on a warmed flour tortilla, sprinkle some grated cheddar cheese over the filling, roll it up and eat it. You can use scrambled eggs instead of meat and beans, too. To get your tortillas warm and soft, heat them on an ungreased surface at a medium high temperature for about thirty seconds on each side.

It's right before midterms, and you're upset, to say the least. It seems your relatives are coming over for dinner against your protests. Weeks ago when you planned this dinner you didn't realize it was going to be in the middle of midterms. Besides, everyone always argues, and it takes hours for your blood pressure to return to normal. You don't need this; what you do need is some peace and quiet. Everyone is counting on you, and you realize you're stuck.

But then a fiendish thought begins to creep into your brain. You may have to have them over, but perhaps you can get them to leave as quickly as possible. Uncle Fester will be there, and he's 375 pounds of solid blob. You know what happens when he gets a bean in him. You know it's a cruel and inhuman thought. You know your apartment is small with no ventilation. But you figure you've been good so far, and God won't punish you for this one. If only the neighbors don't hear the screams and call the police. You go ahead with your fiendish plan; you serve. . .

ALL DAY BAKED BEANS

2 lbs. kidney beans	2 chopped onions
½ lb. bacon	3 tomatoes

Mix a third of the beans and onions in a large (as in "big") casserole dish, and thickly slice one of the tomatoes on top. Repeat twice more until there's no more beans or onions. Bake uncovered at 300 degrees for 2 hours. Cut half the bacon in thirds and lay it on top. Bake for 2 more hours. Stuff the bacon down into the beans and place the other half on top. Bake for a final 2 hours. Get about 5 friends and eat!

Here's one that takes a little bit longer to prepare but is well worth it. Just heat up a can of gravy and pour it over this stuff when you serve it.

YORKSHIRE MEATBALL CASSEROLE

1 lb. ground round	1 cup milk
1 pkg. onion soup mix	2 tbls. butter
4 eggs	1 cup sifted flour
sprinkle of parsley flakes	1 tsp. baking soda
2 tbls. ketchup	½ tsp. salt
pinch of pepper	

Mix the meat, onion soup mix, 1 egg, ketchup, pepper, and parsley flakes. Shape into meatballs and place in shallow casserole dish or pan. Beat 3 eggs until foamy. Add in milk, butter, flour, baking soda, and salt. Beat again until well blended and pour over meat. Bake at 350 degrees for 50 to 60 minutes. Serve with the hot gravy.

ZESTY CHILI MACARONI

1½ lbs. beef rump or chuck, cubed	½ cup grated cheddar cheese
1 8 oz. pkg. elbow macaroni	1 18 oz. can tomato juice
1 can red kidney beans	1 large onion, chopped
1½ tbls. chili powder	2 slices bacon
1 tsp. salt	

Fry the bacon, remove the pieces and leave the fat. Brown the cubed beef and onion. Add the tomato juice, chili powder, salt, and kidney beans. Bring to a boil, reduce heat, and simmer for 1 hour. While that's cooking, cook the macaroni according to package directions. Mix the bacon, macaroni, and meat sauce together and throw into a greased casserole dish. Sprinkle the cheese on top and broil until it melts.

Your roommate's parents are coming over for dinner and you're wondering what to serve them. There's a knock on the front door. It's them. They squeeze in the front door. The are immense, rotund people and they are moving slowly across the room towards you. She is wearing a large green dress and he is wearing a huge green suit. It dawns on you. You serve. . .

you figure out what to serve stuffed bell peppers!

STUFFED BELL PEPPERS

1½ lbs. ground round	2 handfuls cooked rice
1 large chopped onion	2 tbls. chili powder
1 small can corn	grated cheddar cheese
1 can stewed tomatoes	salt, pepper to taste
5 or 6 whole green peppers	

Brown the meat and onion, add the corn, tomatoes, rice, and chili powder. Salt and pepper to taste. Simmer for at least half an hour (the longer the better). This can be eaten just like it is but it really is meant to be stuffed in cored and cleaned bell peppers that have been dropped in boiling water for seven minutes. Top stuffing with grated cheese and place the stuffed peppers into a pan with one inch of water (to prevent burning on the bottom of the peppers). Bake at 350 degrees for 10 to 15 minutes.

Well, it's the last recipe in the chapter and I have a confession to make. I have never tasted this next recipe. I could give lots of reasons for this neglect but what it "boils" down to is, I can't stand Sloppy Joes. I had them in the fourth grade once in the school cafeteria and I threw up. I think perhaps because of my tender age and tender stomach, I was left with severe psychological scars that remain to this day. In any event, I will never touch them again. I understand, however, that this is a truly good Sloppy Joe recipe and since there are many millions of people who enjoy these things, here's the recipe:

MMMMMMM SLOPPY JOES

1 lb. ground round	1 tsp. paprika
1 6 oz. can tomato paste	½ tsp. garlic powder
1 cup water	1 tbls. flour
¼ cup chopped onion	salt to taste

Brown the crumbled meat. Drain. Throw in everything else and bring to a boil. Reduce heat and simmer for 10 minutes. Serve on a toasted hamburger bun.

OK, you've made it through the first chapter and you've put on 20 pounds. Well, don't worry. There's a chapter on nutrition and dieting later on in the book.

Heavier or not, by now you've seen for yourself that cooking is almost as easy, quicker, and less expensive than getting into your car, driving down to "Greasy's," waiting in line, and buying a double barfburger and driving all the way back home so you can eat it cold. See? You can learn a lot more in college than just why the sky is blue or what inductive thinking is. The preparation of food is a universal reality. After all, we can't live without it. Cooking is considered high on the list of philosophic principles. Why do you think Aristotle and all those other philosophers were always talking about "food for thought"? Talk to your philosophy teacher. . .maybe you can get extra credit for reading this book. And if you think you CAN get extra credit for reading this, send $150 for my book on "Inexpensive land purchases in the swamplands of Florida"!

Main Meats

Main Meats

Some nights you come home after a hard day without lunch and you'd like nothing more than to bite into a nice big piece of juicy meat. But you've got this roast you bought sitting in the refrigerator and you just don't know what to do with it. Perhaps it's not roast, but chicken or lamb chops or some other meat. The point is, you're not sure how to cook it and make it taste good. Sure, you can paste some barbecue sauce on almost anything and throw it on the grill and it'll still taste OK. But it's raining outside and you heard somewhere that barbecues act as lightning rods. The answer to your dilemma is in this chapter. In it, I have tried to list at least a couple of ways to prepare most major meats, fish, and poultry. Suppose you should win a Thanksgiving turkey. And you don't know what to do with it. Or suppose you discover that chicken is about the cheapest way to go—but you've had it broiled 27 days in a row. How do you cook these things? The answers to these problems and others appear in the next several pages.

Beef

Besides being the nickname of a guy I knew at school, beef is probably the main ingredient in most students' diets (i.e., the hamburger). There are a couple of important things to remember when buying and preparing beef. When buying your meat, such as steaks, roasts, or other cuts, you must keep in mind that meat containing a good portion of interior fat (marbling) is usually more tender than meat containing little fat. Too often the tendency is to stay away from meat that is marbled because it is ugly or awful looking which is hardly sound reasoning. When cooking these meats it is important to leave the fat on. You don't have to eat it and you can always trim the fat off later, but while cooking the fat retains the juices, thus contributing flavor to the meat. As a result, the meat does not dry out and it tastes much better.

Steaks, of course, are easy. You can broil them three to five inches from the flame, barbecue them, or sprinkle some salt in a thick skillet (to prevent sticking) and pan fry them. But who can afford steak anyway? This section deals mainly with the more or less common meat dishes that are good, fairly easy to prepare, and are inexpensive.

THE ROAST

When cooking the roast, there are a couple of important things to remember. First of all, a small roast requires more minutes per pound of cooking than a larger one. Secondly, a roast should be removed from the oven for about 15 minutes and kept warm before carving. That way, less juice will be lost and the roast will be tastier.

I am assuming that you have already had the tasty rump roast in Chapter 1 and now you are widening your horizons (and hopefully not your waistline) and just itching to taste this delectable delight.

SUPER EASY POT ROAST

2 to 3 lb. pot roast
1 pkg. onion soup mix

2 to 4 good sized potatoes
2 to 4 carrots

Wrap the meat in aluminum foil, with the top left open. Sprinkle onion soup mix on top. Wrap airtight and bake at 350 degrees for 1½ hours. Slice up carrots and potatoes and spread them around the roast. Cook for another hour at 300 degrees.

What do you mean, you cooked the roast and you couldn't eat the whole thing? You're a 5'1", 102 lb. girl and you and your two roommates couldn't eat three pounds of meat and a few potatoes and carrots? Think of the starving people in Asia. What do you mean, if you look at another bite you'll explode? Can you imagine the headlines: "Girl, 18, explodes killing three and injuring several more in bizarre eating orgy?" OK OK. I believe you, save the meat and tomorrow night have the crust casserole in Chapter 1 or hot beef sandwiches.

HOT ROAST BEEF SANDWICHES

leftover roast beef
1 can of mushroom gravy

bread

Thinly slice leftover roast beef and place between two slices of bread like any idiot would make a sandwich. Heat up leftover gravy if there is some, or if not, heat up a can of mushroom gravy and pour piping hot over the sandwich. Good served with peas.

CORNED BEEF

Corned beef is prepared in a brine and salted lightly, giving it that special taste. You either like it or you don't and this recipe won't supply you with any new revelations. Unless you haven't tried eating it smeared with mustard.

CORNED BEEF AND CABBAGE

1 hunk of corned beef
1 rutabaga (yellow turnip)

5 or 6 whole potatoes
1 cabbage

Take the hunk of corned beef and place in a saucepan on top of the stove, covering with water (the corned beef, not the stove). Bring to a boil, reduce heat, and simmer for 4 hours. For the last hour, add 1 peeled and sliced rutabaga (yellow turnip) and five or six whole peeled potatoes. For the last ½ hour, add one quartered cabbage. For an excellent condiment to pour over the cabbage, mix together:

8 oz. cider vinegar   1 tsp. sugar

GROUND BEEF

Usually referred to as ground round or hamburger, ground beef is the main staple of almost all college students. You will notice that virtually half of the recipes in Chapter 1 call for ground round.

There are a couple of things you should keep in mind when you cruise up to the meat section in your local market. First of all, when buying ground round at a bargain price, it's doubtful that it's a bargain. It could be that it's priced for quick sale because it's old. Secondly, there are two grades of ground beef available. The less expensive of the two contains 10% more fat, a good deal of which may melt away during cooking leaving you with less meat than you had anticipated; however, the fat does contribute to the flavor. Following are a number of tasty ground beef dishes.

This first recipe calls for ground round because its cheaper. It's good this way but if you want really good Beef Stroganoff, you can substitute ¾ of a pound of beef sirloin, tenderloin, or round steak cut into bite-sized strips.

BEEF STROGANOFF

8 oz. noodles   2 tsp. flour
1 beef bouillon cube   2 tsp. Worcestershire sauce
6 oz. fresh mushrooms   ½ tsp. garlic
1 lb. ground beef   1 pkg. powdered onion soup mix
1½ cups sour cream   1 cup water
2 tsp. salt

Brown the crumbled meat in butter or cooking oil, drain. Add the flour, salt, mushrooms, garlic, and Worcestershire sauce. Stir slowly for about two minutes. Add powdered onion soup mix and water. Cook on low flame for about 10 minutes. Drop a bouillon cube in boiling water and add your noodles. Add the sour cream to simmering meat sauce and stir in thoroughly. Serve noodles with sauce on top.

LASAGNE

1 lb. ground beef
1 chopped onion
2 10-3/4 oz. cans of tomato soup
1 pint ricotta (or cottage) cheese
½ lb. mozzarella cheese
½ lb. cooked lasagne noodles

½ cup water
2 tsp. vinegar
2 tsp. oregano
garlic salt to taste
parmesan cheese

Cook the lasagne noodles. Brown beef, onion, garlic salt, and oregano. Add soup, water, and vinegar. Bring to a boil, reduce heat, and simmer 30 minutes stirring now and then. In a shallow baking dish, arrange: 1. cooked noodles, 2. ricotta cheese, 3. meat sauce and 4. mozzarella cheese in four alternating layers. Sprinkle with parmesan cheese. Bake for 30 minutes at 350 degrees, letting stand 15 minutes before serving. Note: this tastes better if cooked the night before and reheated when ready to serve. It's good the same day, too.

TAMALE PIE

1½ lbs. ground round
1 chopped onion
2 cans tomato sauce
1 bell pepper chopped

1 small can corn
½ cup diced olives
cornmeal mush

Brown meat and drain. Add onion, tomato sauce, bell pepper, olives, and corn, mixing well. Place a layer of mush on bottom of greased casserole dish. Pour in filling. Place another layer of mush on top. Bake 30 to 45 minutes at 350 degrees.

HAMBURGER SANDWICH

1 loaf French bread
½ to 1 lb. ground beef
½ lb. grated cheese
10 good sized mushrooms
1 cup chopped green pepper

1 cup chopped onion
1½ tsp. oregano
1 lg. can tomato sauce
4 tbls. olive oil (or salad oil)

Slice the bread in half and sprinkle the cheese on top. Place on top of that the crumbled meat, sliced mushrooms, bell pepper, onion, oregano, tomato sauce, and oil (in that order). Place the sandwich on some aluminum foil and stick in the oven at 325 degrees for 20 minutes.

ROLLED MEAT LOAF

2 lbs. ground beef
1 egg
¼ cup water
1 cup crumbled bread
1 chopped onion
2 tsp. salt

¼ tsp. pepper
dash of mace
1 cup peas
1 cup sliced carrots
½ cup crumbled buttered bread

Mix together meat, unbeaten egg, water, crumbled bread, onion, salt, pepper, and mace (if you don't have any mace, just substitute paprika). Spread mixture on a piece of wax paper. Cover with a second piece of wax paper and flatten with a rolling pin. Remove the top paper and spread peas and carrots over mixture. Roll it up like a carpet. Spread buttered crumbs over paper and roll the finished roll back through them. Bake at 350 degrees for 1 hour. This is a good time to toss in a couple of baked potatoes and prepare the entire meal at once.

SPINACH-BEEF POT

1 lb. ground beef
1 10 oz. pkg. frozen spinach
¾ cup sliced fresh mushrooms
1 can stewed tomatoes
1 6 oz. pkg. Noodles Italiano

½ cup grated cheddar cheese
$1/3$ cup wine (red)
pepper, parmesan cheese,
  parsley to taste

Brown meat, drain. Add mushrooms, tomatoes, spinach, wine, and pepper, mixing well. Bring to a boil, reduce heat, and simmer, covered, for 10 minutes. Add the contents from the Noodles Italiano. Mix well and pour in a greased casserole dish. Sprinkle on cheese and parsley. Bake at 375 degrees for 25 minutes.

NIFTY HAMBURGER SAUCE

OK. Lets suppose you've ignored most of this book and have eaten hamburgers 200 days in a row. Here's a nifty hamburger sauce that will spice up the old burger a bit and help you through another 200 days of burger madness. Mix the following ingredients together and slap on that burger.

½ cup blue cheese dressing
½ cup softened butter
¼ tsp. garlic powder

2 tbls. mustard
salt, pepper to taste

HOT DOG

The hot dog is as all-American as the hamburger and there really isn't too much to say about it, except that if you're tired of having them boiled or fried, you can always try them this way.

CHEESE AND BACON DOGS

bacon	hot dogs
1 can baked beans	American cheese

Slice the hot dogs part way lengthwise and stuff with cheese. Wrap a slice of bacon around each dog (holding it on a toothpick) and shove it in the oven at 350 degrees for 20 minutes. In the meantime, heat up that can of beans.

Swine

The swine is a stout-bodied, short-legged, omnivorous mammal with thick bristly skin and a long mobile snout. Sounds pretty appetizing doesn't it. Well, our tasty friend gave us Delicious Spareribs and Ham Dinner in Chapter 1 and promises some more delights here in Chapter 2. As in beef, the flavor of pork comes largely from the fat. When purchasing and cooking pork and ham, it is advantageous to have a good portion of fat in the meat. Ham is a good meat to cook in large amounts because you can always use up the extra in something else delicious. Like it's good fried in the morning with some eggs or in sandwiches. Here's three things to do with ham.

HAM CASSEROLE

2 cups noodles
½ lb. ham, diced
½ lb. cheddar cheese, grated
1 tsp. horseradish sauce

½ tsp. salt
1 can cream of mushroom soup
  or chicken or celery
¼ cup milk

Combine everything together in a buttered, covered, casserole dish. Bake at 350 degrees for 40 minutes. Remove the top and add two slices of buttered cubed bread. Brown under the broiler.

HAM DINNER #2

½ lb. ham, cut in strips
2 tbls. flour
½ cup chopped onion

6 oz. freshly sliced mushrooms
1¼ cup sour cream
½ cup rice

Start cooking the rice, then sauté the ham strips, mushrooms, and onion in butter. Sprinkle in the flour, mixing it well. Stir in the sour cream until it thickens. Pour the sauce over the piping hot rice and serve.

THOSE HOT SUMMER DAYS

This really isn't so much a recipe as a menu selection for one of those days when the heat drives you from the kitchen.

potato salad or macaroni salad
cold sliced ham

sliced avocado
sliced tomatoes

PORK CHOPS

The only important thing you should keep in mind about pork chops is that you should try and get them at least one inch thick. The thinner ones have a tendency to dry out. Here's a couple of good recipes for pork chops, but to be quite frank, one of the best ways to prepare them is Shake' n' Bake. (Don't tell anybody you read it in a cookbook.)

PORK CHOPS AND POTATOES

3 or 4 pork chops
3 or 4 large potatoes

1 can cream of mushroom soup
1/3 can of milk

Grate the large potatoes and lay them in a casserole dish. Pour the soup and milk on top of them, and lay the chops on top of that. Bake in the oven at 350 degrees for ½ hour. Turn the chops over and bake for 30 more minutes.

PORK CHOPS AND ONIONS

4 pork chops	1 tsp. salt
1 cup brown sugar	1 tsp. paprika
1 tsp. dry mustard	1 tbls. water
3 large bermuda onions,	1 tsp. sage
cut in half	½ tsp. pepper

Cook the onions for 10 minutes. Combine remaining ingredients and pour over onions and chops in a baking dish. Bake at 325 degrees for 1 hour, basting often.

Lamb

An interesting thing has been happening on college campuses lately. It seems that a lot of male college students will go to parties in search of an interesting female type. Once he bumps into her, he will take her back to his apartment, prepare her a delicious lamb dinner, and then never see her again. This phenomena is called, "Wham, lamb, thank you ma'am." (Oh well, remember, you didn't buy this book for good jokes, just good recipes.) Here's a couple of good lamb recipes.

RACK OF LAMB

thick lamb chops	ketchup
as many strips of bacon	Worcestershire sauce

Cut away the bones from the chops and wrap a slice of bacon around each piece of lamb securing with a toothpick. Add 1 teaspoon of Worcestershire sauce and ketchup to each one. Cook on a rack with some aluminum foil underneath to catch the drips. Bake at 350 for 35 minutes.

ZUCCHINI CHOPS

4 lamp chops   3 small zucchini, sliced
1 chopped onion   2 tsp. salt
2 tsp. garlic powder   ¼ tsp. pepper

Brown the chops on both sides in oil and remove from the pan. Sauté the onion and zucchini in the same pan. Throw the chops back in along with everything else and cook 10 to 15 minutes, covered, on medium heat.

Domestic Fowl

Chicken and turkey are not meat, of course, but they make such frequent appearances on the table as the main dish that I couldn't help but include them in this chapter.

CHICKEN

Unless you've been away from the planet for awhile, you've probably noticed that chicken is usually less expensive than most cuts of meat. Here's a couple of recipes that will help stretch the budget. If you liked the chicken recipe in Chapter 1, you'll love these.

FRIED CHICKEN

1 cut up chicken   salt, pepper to taste
1 cup flour   shortening

Put the flour, salt, and pepper in a plastic bag. If the chicken isn't moist, moisten it in melted butter. Heat shortening in a large skillet to a depth of one inch. Heat until a drop of water spits at you. Place chicken in pan over moderate heat, skin side down. Cook 10 minutes on each side until brown and crispy.

MUSHROOM CHICKEN

1 cut up chicken   ½ cup chopped onions
1 can cream of mushroom salt
 soup   garlic salt
1 cup milk   paprika

Spread chicken out on a sheet of aluminum foil. Lightly sprinkle with salt, garlic salt, and paprika. Dilute soup with milk and pour over chicken. Sprinkle onions on top. Bake at 350 for 1½ hours.

CHICKEN CASSEROLE

1 cut up chicken   2 chicken bouillon cubes
¾ cup rice (uncooked)   dissolved in 1¾ cup water
½ cup sliced fresh mushrooms flour
1 tbls. grated onion   oil
salt, pepper to taste

Flour and brown chicken in a pan. In a greased casserole dish, mix rice, onion, salt, pepper, mushrooms, bouillon cube, and water. Add browned chicken on top, butter well. Cover, bake at 350 for 1 hour.

OK. You live in Beaver Dam, Wisconsin, attended school in Pasadena, California, and you just can't ride your ten speed home and back during the four day weekend. You have a couple of friends in the same boat. You invite them over and you whip up a turkey. What's that? You mean you don't know how to WHIP up a turkey? All right, all right, that's what I'm here for. The first thing you have to do is thaw the thing (if it's frozen). It takes about a day for a 4 to 12 pound bird, a day and a half for a 12 to 20 pound bird and 2 days for a 20 to 400 pound bird. It's very important that the turkey be thawed. A turkey that has not been thawed prior to cooking will not cook correctly and will not taste good. After thawing the turkey, wash and dry the cavity. Place a prepared dressing (Mom's Best) in body and neck cavity. Wrap the turkey thoroughly in aluminum foil, leaving a narrow slit at the top, two inches long. All you have to do now is cook it. A good guideline for cooking turkey is to cook it about 20 minutes per pound for a bird 16 pounds or less, 15 minutes per pound for larger birds. To test for doneness, grasp the drumstick by the end and move it gently. If it moves easily or breaks away, the bird is done. When it is finally cooked, let the turkey juices settle for 20 minutes before carving.

Everyone thinks their mom's dressing is the best and I'm no exception.

MOM'S BEST TURKEY DRESSING

1 doz. stale hamburger buns	1 celery stalk chopped fine
1 large onion chopped fine	1½ tsp. sage
½ cup orange juice	salt, pepper to taste

Mix everything together and place in the body and neck cavity of the bird, securing with skewers.

Fish

Fish, like domestic fowl, is not a meat as such. But it does pop up now and then as the main course (twice in Chapter 1). If you're Catholic, you've probably had it a million different ways a million different times and possibly could care less if you ever see another fishy again. Regardless of your religious convictions, here's an easy fish recipe along with three tuna recipes. Tuna, of course, is one of the stalwarts of the economy menu.

2ND EASIEST FISH RECIPE IN THE WORLD

4 filets   1 can of shrimp soup

Place the fish in a shallow, greased baking dish. Bake it at 400 for 20 minutes. Warm up the soup and pour it over the fish. Bake both for 10-12 minutes at 300. Serve with lemon or the fish sauce in Chapter 6.

IF YOU'RE INTO TUNA

7½ oz. can of tuna   2 eggs
1 green pepper, chopped   1 can creamed corn
1 medium sized onion, chopped   1 can evaporated milk

Beat the eggs and mix with evaporated milk. Add in remaining ingredients, mix well, and dump into a buttered casserole dish. Bake uncovered at 325 for 1 hour.

TUNA BAKE

¼ cup chopped onion   8 oz. macaroni (cooked and
1 can undiluted mushroom   drained)
   soup   1 can of tuna
1 pkg. of cream cheese,   1 pkg. frozen peas (cooked and
   cubed   drained)
salt, pepper to taste   ¼ cup stuffed olives (if you
                                     have them)

Combine everything but the cheese in a casserole dish, mixing well. Spread the cheese over top. Bake at 350 for 30 minutes.

TUNA #4

1 can cream of celery soup	1 can tuna
1/3 cup milk	touch of soy sauce
1 chopped green pepper	1 can chow mein noodles
celery, chopped	

Mix everything but the noodles, heat both and serve the mix over the noodles.

I hate to be sexist but this is probably a male-only recipe. Finals are over and you've been out celebrating. You've had about 18 beers and quite frankly, you're in an incoherent stupor. As is usual, after you've been drinking for about 12 hours, you start to get hungry. You would like to go get something to eat but you know you shouldn't drive in this state (or in any other state for that matter) and besides, you're stuck under the coffee table at your friend's house. Looking around from your vantage point, you see shapes darting back and forth only a few feet away. Focusing through the blur that used to be 20-20 vision, you recognize your friend's aquarium within reach. You have...

TASTY GOLDFISH DELIGHT

a friendship,	1 aquarium, full of fish
on the rocks anyway.	

You net or grab the slippery little monsters as quickly as you can before they go into shock and die. If, because of your temporary lack of hand-eye coordination, you can't seem to grab them, just figure some way to get the water out of the tank; out of the water the fish are easier to catch. Once you get one, just swallow him whole. (NOTE: Perhaps Dad has some nifty recipes from his college days.)

Vegetables, Potatoes, and other Dinner Accessories

Vegetables, Potatoes, and other Dinner Accessories

Quite a few meals like chili, spaghetti, or casseroles really don't need any vegetables or potatoes with them. They're good by themselves. Other meals like fish and pot roast need trimmings to go along with them. That's what this chapter is all about; things to eat with your main dish. In the next few pages, I've described some vegetable dishes that take a little thought, some interesting potato ideas, and a number of good ways to liven up rice.

Vegetables

Many of the salad-type vegetables are not mentioned in this chapter but are saved for the next one. There are also many vegetables that you can buy frozen or fresh and boil according to package directions until they are tender. Those aren't in here either. There is no sense in telling you how to do something you can read on a package. There are just a couple of things I would like to mention in regard to boiling vegetables and they are the following:

53

1. Do not salt vegetables while cooking them. Salt draws the vitamins out of the vegetables.
2. Cook vegetables in as little liquid as possible. Actually, the best thing you could do is invest a few dollars in a little vegetable steamer basket. They're quite inexpensive and fit right in any saucepan. A few advantages to steaming vegetables: You retain the water-soluble vitamins, B and C, the natural flavor, and a crispy texture of the vegetables. In addition, they take half the time to cook than if you had boiled them.

But knowing human nature and the fact that most people will probably ignore what I've just said, or don't care about vitamins anyway, most of these recipes that call for boiling are left that way. They will still taste good and will be good for you but not as good as they would be steamed.

It's probably a good idea to buy those big bags of corn, peas, green beans, and other vegetables that you find in the frozen food section. That way you can use them in whatever amounts you need and just seal the rest back in the bag. Cans, on the other hand, once open must be eaten right away or thrown out. In any event, here are some good vegetables that aren't too ordinary.

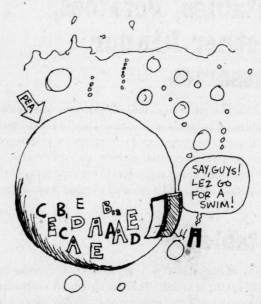

WHAT HAPPENS WHEN YOU USE TOO MUCH WATER

FRIED ZUCCHINI

Melt 2 tbls. of butter over low heat in a pan. Add a package of frozen zucchini or thinly sliced fresh zucchini. Cover, and simmer about 20 minutes. Remove the cover and turn up the heat stirring occasionally 'till each piece is lightly browned. Zucchini is done when a fork easily pierces the center.

ZUCCHINI #2

¼ cup water   salt, pepper to taste
. ¼ cup chopped onion   2 tbls. butter
½ cup sour cream   5 zucchini squashes

Grate the zucchini squashes and cook them in boiling water for 5 minutes. Drain and mix in everything else. Bring back up to a near boil and serve.

BELL (OR ACORN) SQUASH

Slice the squash in quarters and clean out the seeds. Butter the insides and poke little holes in to let the steam escape. Bake at 350 for 1½ hours.

RUTABAGA (TURNIP)

Have you ever heard of anyone falling off the rutabaga truck? Of course not. However, I am informed that this vegetable is referred to as a rutabaga in proper circles. Not being too proper, I prefer the name turnip. Either way, peel and dice the selected amount of vegetable and cook in about ½ cup water 25 to 30 minutes until tender. Drain, mash, and add 1 level tsp. of sugar per turnip. Serve smothered in butter.

This is a good recipe if you're baking something else; you can just throw these right in with it.

BAKED CARROTS

5 or 6 carrots   butter
2 tbls. water

Slice up the carrots very thin and place them in a small casserole dish. Dot them generously with butter and bake at 325 for 40 minutes.

CORN ON THE COB

I know corn on the cob may seem simple to a lot of people, but there must be somebody else out there who at one time didn't know how to cook it. Can you believe when I first moved away I had to call Mom long distance so she could tell me just how simple it is to prepare corn on the cob? You just fill a pan with enough water to cover the corn. Get the water boiling and submerge the frozen or fresh ears. Cook frozen corn about 10 minutes, fresh corn only about 2 minutes.

Potatoes

THE POTATO
SPUD OF MANY
TALENTS

Potatoes really need no introduction. They have got to be the best dinner accessory ever invented. Hardly a meal goes by that is not accompanied by french fries, potato chips, potato salad, or a baked potato. Here's eleven good ways to prepare potatoes.

BAKED POTATO

Baked potatoes are great. You just wash them, poke a few holes through them and pop them in the oven with that roast or anything else you might have cooking. Bake them at 400 for 40 minutes, 375 for one hour, 325 for 1½ hours or 170 for three weeks.

THE BOILED POTATO

I was never a big fan of boiled potatoes myself but there are people who enjoy them immensely. Knowing how to boil potatoes is important because boiling is the first step for various other potato recipes. You simply peel and quarter as many potatoes as desired and place them in a deep pan filled with lightly salted water. Bring the water to a boil, cover, and turn down the heat, cooking for 20 to 25 minutes. Drain and serve, smothered in butter and with salt and pepper. Or, you can have. . .

MASHED POTATOES

Just cook the boiled potatoes as above. Drain them and mash them adding a little milk until creamy. Or, you can have. . .

ONION POTATOES

Brown a chopped onion. Take the boiled, mashed potatoes and mix them in with the onion. Place in a greased casserole dish and bake at 350 for 45 minutes. Or, if you like cheese, you can try. . .

CHEESY TATERS

Just take the potatoes you have just boiled and mashed and place them in a greased casserole dish. Grate some cheddar cheese on top and sprinkle with parsley flakes. Bake uncovered at 350 for 15 minutes. Or you can save your leftover mashed potatoes and tomorrow you can have. . .

POTATO PANCAKES

You can, of course, use freshly mashed potatoes that have cooled down. Either way, mix in with your mashed potatoes some onion (chopped) and one beaten egg. Shape into patties and fry in butter at a medium temperature until brown. Or you can just use your leftover boiled potatoes and make. . .

FRIED SLICED POTATOES

Just take those leftover boiled potatoes or boiled potatoes that have cooled down and slice them ¼ to ½ inch thick. Pre-heat a grill or frying pan and grill the slice of potato in lots of melted butter. You onion fans can slice some onions in rings and add them in. Salt and pepper to taste. NOTE: Don't stack the potatoes while cooking them but turn them individually allowing each slice to get browned thoroughly. Or you can have. . .

POTATO SALAD

Use the potatoes you have just boiled and drained. Add in some chopped green onion and Miracle Whip to coat. Salt and pepper to taste. Place in the refrigerator to cool. Eat later on, as it's better when cool.

Well, so much for the derivatives of the boiled potato. Now on to some other goodies.

FRENCH FRIES

Melt cooking oil two inches deep in a saucepan until a drop of water will spit at you. Peel and cut the desired amount of potatoes and immerse them in the hot oil. Fry until done, keeping the flame at a medium temperature. Drain on paper towels and serve.

SCALLOPED POTATOES

potatoes
¾ cup milk

grated cheddar cheese
chopped onion

In a greased casserole dish place a layer of thinly sliced potatoes. Salt and pepper them lightly, sprinkle some grated cheddar cheese, chopped onion, and a couple of small chunks of butter over the top—in that order. (Repeat if necessary with more layers of same.) Finally, pour milk on top and bake uncovered for 1½ hours at 350.

MUSHROOM TATERS

Shred 4 medium-sized potatoes and place in the bottom of a casserole dish. Mix one can of mushroom soup with half a can of milk, heat up and pour over the potatoes. Bake at 350 for 1¾ hours. Throw in a few freshly sliced mushrooms if you have them.

Rice

HALF THE WORLD'S POPULATION'S
MAIN DIET IS RICE.

For over half of the world's population, rice is the main ingredient in the diet. It is a nutritious food that's inexpensive and is quite delicious. There are two kinds of rice, white and brown. These recipes deal with white rice. Brown rice is more nutritious but a little more expensive and requires a different cooking method. When cooking any amount of rice, all you have to remember is two thirds water and one third rice. Just lightly salt the water, throw in the rice and follow the directions. Serve the rice plain, topped with butter, or with Worcestershire sauce as a seasoning. Another tasty alternative is to substitute tomato juice for half of the water—it tastes good buttered. If you have any leftover rice that's already cooked, you can fry it up with some chopped onions—it makes a good snack. You can also try the following rice recipes.

ONION RICE

1 can onion soup   1 cup water
1 cup rice

Mix everything together and cook over medium heat 20 to 25 minutes.

RICE #2

1^1/$_3$ cup rice   ¼ cup chopped onions
¼ cup almonds   ¼ cup mushrooms
¼ cup raisins

Cook the rice. Sauté the onions, almonds, and mushrooms. Mix everything together and serve.

CHEESE RICE

1 cup rice   2 cup water
3 tbls. butter ^{1}/$_3$ cup grated cheese (cheddar
pepper to taste   or Monterey jack)

Cook the rice in the butter and lightly salted water as you normally would. Five minutes before it's done, sprinkle the grated cheese over top and lightly pepper to taste.

SPANISH RICE

1 cup rice   2 cups water
3 slices crumbled bacon   1 can tomato sauce
1 tbls. oil   1 tsp. salt
¼ cup chopped celery   1 tsp. garlic salt
¼ cup chopped onion   1 4 oz. can diced green chiles

Brown the bacon and drain. Mix in together the oil, celery, and onion. Sauté until brown. Now add the water, tomato sauce, salt, and garlic salt. Bring to a boil, add the rice, and bring to a boil again. Reduce heat, cover, and simmer for 20 minutes. Finally add in the bacon and chiles, serve.

Appetizer, The

I know what you're thinking. If this is such a quick and easy recipe book, why for heaven's sake is there an appetizer section? I mean come on. When you're eating by yourself, you don't start out with a few drinks, a little music, then an appetizer, three courses, a big dessert and follow it with a few more drinks and then into your room for a little nookie-nookie. No, you wolf down the chow and then get back to whatever you were doing. Well, this is so good, I just had to leave it in here. I call it an appetizer because if I have a few friends over and we get hungry for a little snack late at night, I just whip this up and we eat it and then we're really hungry. . .

THE PERFECT COMBO

NACHOS

tortilla chips
chopped onion
chopped bell pepper
grated Monterey jack cheese
grated cheddar cheese

Spread the tortilla chips evenly over one or more pie plates, about 1½ layers deep. Sprinkle over the chopped onion, bell pepper, and grated cheeses. Heat in oven until the cheese melts. A delicious midnight snack or pre-dinner appetizer.

So much for the trimmings. There are a few things I didn't mention, like homemade Bisquick biscuits being really good, but I figured you can probably read boxes and understand them all by yourself. Besides, you didn't buy a cookbook to read about something you don't have to be Sherlock Holmes to figure out on your own.

Salads, A Word on Nutrition and some Vegetarian Dishes

Salads

One of the most nutritious and best things you can possibly eat is the salad. The salad is packed full of vitamins and is hardly fattening at all. Carrots, lettuce, and other ingredients are good roughage items that help clean out your system. Fruit and vegetable salads whose ingredients are in season are cheaper, easier to prepare, and better for you than just about anything else. For most salads, all you have to remember is to wash everything thoroughly and toss them in together. Washing everything is very important because of the insecticides used to treat everything nowadays. If you've ever been up at 2 a.m. some night and have turned on the tube you know there's always some mutant movie about the residents of some small town that inhale deadly insecticide gas or just plain don't wash their vegetables. Of course, that probably doesn't happen in real life, but there's no sense being a mutant if you don't have to be.

So, if anybody can make a salad, what's this chapter all about anyway? Well, in the next few pages, I have named most of the popular ingredients that would go into both fruit and tossed vegetable salads. Some are old familiar friends and some may be brand new to you. Don't be afraid to experiment; I wouldn't tell you to try something that wasn't delicious, now would I? There is also a list of herbs and spices that often adds to salads, and a few homemade dressings that have no preservatives.

TOSSED VEGETABLE SALAD

Vegetable salads are easy; you've eaten them often, I'm sure. Here's a tip: Tear up leafy greens like they do in the best restaurants instead of cutting them up. This helps the leaves hold the dressing rather than have it all drip to the bottom of the bowl. Of course, wash everything thoroughly first. Following are a list of the more common ingredients in tossed vegetable salads.

ALFALFA SPROUTS - These young green sprouts taste like grass to some people. Just wash them, drain, and toss in a salad as is.

ANCHOVIES - These are just small, tasty fish. Drain them first, then sprinkle on your salad.

ARTICHOKE HEARTS - You can put these in sliced or unsliced. Either way, they are a delicious, nutritious addition to any salad.

ASPARAGUS BITS - Cook the fresh/frozen asparagus, tips up, in boiling water until barely tender. Drain, break off the tough end of stalk, and add into salad.

AVOCADO - This is the best ingredient ever invented; they are literally packed with vitamins. Make sure they are ripe, otherwise they are no good and not very tasty. They must be soft and dark. Putting them in a paper bag helps ripen them faster. Avocado can be kept from discoloring by adding lemon juice to the soft inner fruit.

BEANSPROUTS - These crunchy sprouts should be washed and added to salad, seeds and all. Don't look at them, just eat them.

BEET GREENS - These tasty greens must be tender, young, and clean. Break into small bits and throw in salad.

BELL PEPPERS - Wash and discard the stem and seeds of these crunchy peppers. They are good chopped up or thinly sliced.

BERMUDA ONIONS - A large, mild, white or light yellow onion. Should be peeled and sliced thin crosswise. Separate into rings. If you want to be clever you can cut them into triangles.

BIBB LETTUCE - Sometimes called limestone lettuce, it has dark green leaves that have a very delicate flavor.

BUTTERHEAD LETTUCE - Often called Boston lettuce, its pale green leaves are not as crisp as other lettuce.

CARROT STRIPS - Just grab one of those long orange things that Bugs Bunny is always gnawing on, peel away the outside and thinly slice it into 4-inch long strips.

CELERY - Chopped celery adds crunchiness to any salad but it doesn't absorb dressing and all the pieces end up in the bottom of the bowl.

CHEESE - Thinly sliced or grated cheddar, Swiss, Monterey jack, or other types of cheeses are always good.

CROUTONS - Small cubes of bread either toasted or fried in butter or oil (play your cards right and you can read the easy crouton recipe at the end of this section).

CUCUMBERS - Wash the cucumber and thinly slice it with the skin still on. Add it, as is, into the salad.

DANDELION GREENS - If you're adventurous, early in the spring is a good time to gather tiny green dandelions...yes, right off the lawn. You can cut them apart, wash them well, and add the leaves to your salad. (In gourmet circles, this is in.)

I just had a thought here. It's funny how much of eating and living is just conditioning. Suppose you went into an expensive French restaurant and the waiter said: "Monsieur, Mademoiselle, ze dandelion greens have been plucked at ze exact moment of tenderness and flown here from Paris to be added into your salad zis evening." You would probably be very impressed and say "oh, wow, great." But, if your little brother came in the house on a Saturday afternoon with a few dandelions he saved from the lawnmower clutched in his dirty hand and said, "Think these will be OK in tonight's salad?" your reaction might be quite different.

ENDIVE LETTUCE - A bunchy head lettuce with curly leaves; this green has a pleasantly bitter flavor.

ESCAROLE - Part of the endive family, the broad, curly leaves on this green make it a good base for a tossed salad.

GREEN ONIONS - Remove the roots and all but about two inches of the leaves. Remove the outside layer and chop this onion into little bits and toss into the salad.

ICEBERG LETTUCE - This is the most popular lettuce in America. Its very crisp, pale green leaves make an excellent base for any salad.

ITALIAN ONIONS - Large, mild red onions with big noses and hairy arm pits. Peel, slice thin crosswise, and separate into rings.

KALE - Trim the tough stems and bruised or wilted leaves off this curly, leaved member of the cabbage family.

LEAF LETTUCE - This soft, leaved lettuce was first brought to America by Leaf Erikson. It's best when young and very tender, making a good base for any salad.

LEEKS - Cut this member of the onion family into sections, then halve lengthwise and separate layers. Throw into salad as is.

MANDARIN ORANGE SEGMENTS - These come in a can, and are especially good with vinegar and oil dressing. Just drain the segments and toss into the salad.

MUSHROOMS - Fresh mushrooms are very flavorful, but be sure and wash them thoroughly if you know what's good for you. Trim the bottom off the stems and peel only if the skins are discolored. Cut into thin slices.

PARSLEY - Discard the coarse stems and sprinkle the leaves over salad (see herbs).

RADISHES - Some people like these in their salads but their texture is such that the dressing runs off them and the cut parts end up in the bottom of the bowl. Nobody I know wants three mouthfuls of radishes at the end of their salad.

ROAD APPLES - Not a good idea to use these in a salad at all.

ROMAINE - The finest of the lettuce family, Romaine has long green leaves that crisp easily. It has a slightly stronger flavor than iceberg.

SCALLIONS - A member of the onion family, scallions should be chopped fine and sprinkled over the salad.

SHALLOTS - Like the scallions, shallots are a member of the onion family and are just fine chopped up and sprinkled on top of the salad.

SPANISH ONIONS - Large mild-flavored yellow or white onions. They should be sliced thin crosswise and separated into rings.

SPINACH LEAVES - Fresh, raw spinach leaves well washed and crisped are delicious. A serious side effect of eating lots of this green, however, is that you develop big forearms and calves and start to swear and smoke a corncob pipe. The tatoos that appear with this malady can also be embarrassing.

SWISS CHARD - Leaves like spinach but better tasting than spinach (and without the adverse side effects). A good green as a base or with iceberg lettuce.

TOMATOES - The "T" in "BLT." Tomatoes should be sliced, halved, and added just before serving. If they are put in too soon, they make the salad soggy and dilute the dressing. The small, cherry tomatoes are really best for salads.

WATERCRESS - Cloverlike and dark green leaved, watercress should be washed thoroughly and added to the salad as whole sprigs.

Now that you have your tossed vegetable salad, how about some herbs and spices to add in (one or two at the most).

HERBS AND SPICES

I would like to mention that herbs and spices are not just meant for salads, but for all foods. However, as they do affect the taste of a dish, and taste is largely a matter of opinion, I leave the discovery of what herbs and spices suit which dishes up to the individual. I have listed here just the herbs and spices one would find suitable to tossed green salads. Herbs and spices should be tried one at a time, a little at a time.

BASIL - This basically delicately-flavored herb has medium-size, wide, green leaves that should be washed, chopped up, and sprinkled in food lightly.

CAPERS - Not something Batman investigates, these delicious tiny flower buds of the caper plant are great in salads.

CHERVIL - This member of the carrot family has tasty, delicately-flavored leaves.

CHIVES - This mild form of onion should be washed and chopped up fine before sprinkling on salad. Chives can be found growing wild in baked potatoes and sour cream.

DILL - The fernlike leaves chopped up are used much the same way chives are and are just as good on salads.

GARLIC - This herb is best used for salads by taking a halved clove and rubbing the salad bowl well. Never put garlic directly into a salad.

GROUND PEPPER - If you're not getting enough taste out of your pepper, try freshly ground pepper. The taste and aroma is stunningly superior to pre-ground pepper.

MARJORAM - This small leaved member of the mint family has a very strong flavor and should be used very lightly.

MINT - You know, of course, what mint tastes like, but did you know it's also delicious lightly sprinkled in salads?

MUSTARD - If you've ever had a hot dog you probably know what mustard tastes like, right? Well, the leaves of the mustard plant can be added to salads with a light hand to give the salad a slightly different kind of taste.

OREGANO - These oval-shaped leaves are quite strong and should be used lightly. . .a little goes a long way.

PARSLEY - This herb is loaded with vitamins and minerals. Its small, green leaves are found growing wild on plates in most restaurants. They should be picked and washed thoroughly (no telling where they've been), chopped up and added to the salad.

ROSEMARY - The very thin leaves of this herb have a very distinct flavor and should be used sparingly.

THYME — Again, another strongly-flavored herb that should be used in small amounts.

The salad is not complete without a dressing. I've included a couple of dressings here that you can make yourself. Of course buying a bottle of dressing is easier but in making it, you have the advantage of wholesome ingredients and no preservatives. . .and, it's cheaper. Vinegar and oil is the easiest of all dressings, just remember two parts olive oil and one part vinegar. The reverse is deadly.

HONEY LIME DRESSING

Simply thin honey to taste with lime juice.

FRENCH DRESSING

Mix together:
4 tbls. vinegar
½ cup olive oil

$2/3$ tsp. salt
¼ tsp. pepper
a dash of dry mustard

TOMATO DRESSING

Mix together:
3 whole green onions, chopped
3 sprigs parsley, chopped fine
2 tomatoes, diced

1 cup sour cream
¼ tbls. parmesan
1 tsp. paprika
1 tbls. vinegar

THE SAN DIEGAN

½ cup tarragon vinegar
¼ cup water
1½ tbls. lemon juice

1 tbls. brown sugar
½ tsp. salt

Here's that easy crouton recipe I promised earlier.

EASY CROUTON RECIPE

¼ cup olive oil
½ tsp. garlic powder

4 slices diced bread

Simmer oil and garlic until hot. Add the bread squares and brown over a low flame, making sure to coat each square well. Drain the croutons on some paper towels. You can store these forever in a jar in the refrigerator.

FRUIT SALAD

Fruit salad, like tossed vegetable salad, is really easy to make, good for you, and very inexpensive when you compare nutrients to dollars. As long as there isn't a freeze or something, fruits are usually quite easily accessible. Unlike tossed vegetable salad however, you probably haven't eaten a million fruit salads. They're really easy to make—you just mix two cups any fruit mixture with ¼ cup confectioners sugar and stick it in the refrigerator for a little while. Three kinds of fruit is usually plenty, but you can add more if it's the right combination. Too much variety is not always the spice of life when it comes to fruit salads. You can eat the salad out of bowls or if you're having someone special over and you want to be fancy, you can serve it in hollowed-out melon halves. Here is a list of things that go nicely in fruit salads.

APPLES - Wash thoroughly, peel, and cut into quarters, remove core and put in as is or dice. Toss in with pineapple or citrus fruit to prevent discoloring.

AVOCADOS - These are really best in vegetable salad but can be used in fruit salads, too. Cut lengthwise, remove the seed (as if I had to tell you) and dig out the fruit with a spoon. Lemon juice will help prevent discoloring.

BANANAS - Like apples, sliced bananas should be tossed with a citrus fruit or pineapple to prevent discoloring.

BLUEBERRIES - Sort and rinse the berries, drain and add as is into salad.

CANTALOUPE - Cut cantaloupe in quarters. Remove seeds, cut away rind, and thinly slice.

CHERRIES - Sort, rinse, and drain fruit. Remove stems, cut into halves, and remove pits. Pitted black cherries just need to be rinsed.

GRAPEFRUIT - Rinse fruit, cut away peel and white membrane. Remove sections by breaking apart or cutting away and remove any seeds. Out-of-season frozen grapefruit sections are great.

HONEYDEW MELON - Cut the melon in half, remove the seeds, and using a spoon, dig out little melon balls. They deliciously sweeten up any salad.

MANDARIN ORANGE SEGMENTS - These usually come in cans so it's easy to remove them from the can, drain them, and put them right in the salad.

NECTARINES - Rinse the nectarines, cut them into halves, remove the pits, and dice them up.

ORANGES - Rinse the fruit, cut away peel and white membrane. Remove sections by breaking apart or cutting away and remove any seeds.

PEACHES - Plunge the fruit into boiling water then into cold water. Gently slip off the skins and dice the fruit. Mix with citrus fruit (pineapple is a good choice) to prevent discoloring.

PEARS - Wash fruit thoroughly, peel, and cut into quarters. Remove core and add in as is or dice. As with many other fruits, it's a good idea to mix pears with citrus fruit to prevent them from turning brown.

PINEAPPLES - Cut off the spiny top and discard. Rinse fruit and cut into crosswise slices. Cut away and discard rind and eyes. Cut away core and finally cut rings into wedges or chunks.

PLUMS - Simply rinse the plums, cut them in half, and remove the pits.

RED RASPBERRIES - Sort and rinse the berries and toss them right in.

STRAWBERRIES - Sort, rinse, and drain the berries. The hull can be removed or left on for garnish. If you're eating by yourself and don't have anyone to impress, just pull them off.

WHITE SEEDLESS GRAPES - Rinse and drain thoroughly. Reduce the large bunches into small clusters so they mix around well.

MACARONI SALAD, THE

This salad is so tasty that I just had to make a special section for it—it couldn't be left out. This can be used as a main dish or with a main dish, depending on how hungry you are.

MARY'S MACARONI SALAD

1 small pkg. salad macaroni	½ pint sour cream
1 chopped onion	4 tbls. vinegar
2 tbls. salad oil	2 jars chopped pimento
sprinkle parsley flakes	1½ cup chopped celery
salt, pepper to taste	¾ cup pickle relish

Cook and drain the salad macaroni, let cool about half an hour (you can run them under cold water to speed process). Mix vinegar and salad oil very well. Add everything else making sure it's cold before adding sour cream (or it will melt). Place in the refrigerator until ready to use. It's better after a day or two.

Nutrition

The more you cook, the more you will probably start looking at what you eat. You just might start looking at things like vitamins, minerals, and fats. Eventually, you start to get concerned with the nutritional value of the things you eat. That's why in various sections of this book I have leaned towards items like fresh vegetables rather than canned ones, dressings without preservatives, and occasional thoughts on "junk food." The way a great deal of people visualize eating is that the human stomach should not be a battleground between the forces of nutrition and garbage. One should be in harmony with one's digestive system. Your body is like a machine; if you don't give it the right fuel, it doesn't work right and it runs down quicker.

If you have looked into the nutritional value of the various foods in your diet, chances are you've thought about health foods and possibly even dieting a little. The proper diet, healthy foods, and dieting all work hand in hand. If you're overweight, you're probably not in the greatest shape and most of it has to do with your diet. Now I'm no expert and I'm not advocating anything but it's my book and I'm going to get in my two cents' worth. I have read a few things about nutrition and I have had a little experience in that department. I know for sure that America doesn't get all the vitamins it should be getting. I also know that vitamins are essential to your body for good health and that they are contained in almost everything we eat. I'm not going to go on and on and tell you what vitamins are good for what, but I am going to include a recipe for a health milkshake if you're curious enough to try it.

A HEALTH MILKSHAKE

1½ cups nonfat milk	3 tbls. lecithin
3 scoops honey ice cream	3 tbls. carob powder
3 tbls. yeast	

Everything should be in a blender and mixed well. The yeast and lecithin are both very good for you, carob is a natural chocolate, milk mixes everything together, and the honey ice cream kills the taste. This is breakfast (with a few vitamin tablets) for me. It's much better for you than coffee, and hardly fattening at all (except for the ice cream)!

While I'm rambling on here, I'm going to get a word in on dieting: "exercise." That's right, exercise. It just about makes me sick when I see people go on these fad diets. The best thing to do is eat the right kind of things and exercise—your body will do the rest. I'm no gem myself but I did wrestle in high school and college and nobody knows how to diet like wrestlers. I used to lose four pounds a day from a 5'10" 142 pound frame and then eat it back on at night. But I was in great shape from exercising all the time and eating the right kinds of foods. Now I know you're busy with school and all and it's a lot of trouble to do those sit ups and then run around the block chased by savage dobermans and tripping over sprinklers. But just think if you're worried now, wait until you're 35 years old. You're supposed to be in the prime of life and there you sit and cram Twinkies in your mouth while you complain about having to go on another diet. If you don't like my exercise idea and you're really desperate, you can eat things like hard boiled eggs and drink apple and other citrus juices. A hard boiled egg has only 80 calories and your body burns up 92 calories digesting it. Apple and citrus juices work on much the same principle. Sooooo, if you eat about 25 hard boiled eggs per day, your body will use up a whopping 250 calories a day. Me—I'd rather exercise.

Some Vegetarian Dishes

More and more people today are turning towards vegetarian diets than ever before. I thought it would be appropriate to include a couple of tasty vegetarian dishes here in the salad section, as vegetables are what most vegetarians eat. (Hence the name, "vegetarian." Pretty clever, don't you think?) There are basically two types of vegetarians; people who have decided they are not going to eat meat, and pure vegetarians, who not only do not eat meat, but also milk or milk products. If you are in the first group, then you appreciated the vegedilla, mushroom casserole, and other recipes in Chapter 1. If you are in the latter group, then you already know what you're doing and odds are, you're not even reading this, so I'm just going to ignore you for the remainder of this book.

The rest of the world is way ahead of us in vegetarian recipes. The Chinese, Mexican, Japanese, and Italian diets, among others, contain numerous non-meat dishes. Following are a few vegetarian recipes from around here that are in keeping with the theme of this book, that is, easy, inexpensive, and good to eat.

SOOO YOU DON'T EAT MEAT BECAUSE IT'S A LIVING THING?

BEAN NUT LOAF

1 chopped bell pepper	1 cup cooked, dried beans
2 chopped celery stalks	1 cup chopped walnuts
1 tsp. chopped parsley	1 beaten egg
¼ tsp. paprika	1 cup tomatoes
1 tsp. Worcestershire sauce	1 cup bread crumbs
1 tsp. horseradish sauce	1 cup chopped onion

Sauté the onion, bell pepper, and celery. Mix together with everything else in a greased loaf pan. Bake at 375 for 30 minutes.

CASHEW RICE LOAF

2 cups chopped raw cashews
2 cups brown rice, cooked
2 cups milk
2 chopped onions
4 slices crumbled wheat bread

4 tbls. oil
4 tbls. parsley
2 tbls. soy sauce
½ tbls. thyme or sage
salt to taste

Throw everything together, mixing well, and bake covered for one hour at 350.

VEGETARIAN CHOW MEIN

3 cups sliced celery
2 cups sliced onion
2 cups bean sprouts
1 cup sliced mushrooms
¼ cup parsley

1½ cups water
3 tbls. oil
1¼ tbls. arrowroot starch
½ tsp. onion powder
½ tsp. salt

Toss the oil, ¼ cup water, salt, and onion powder in a large skillet. Add in the vegetables and heat covered until tender (about 15 minutes). Toss in the parsley, the rest of the water, ¼ tsp. salt and the arrowroot starch. Heat up until nicely hot, serve over hot brown rice with soy sauce. Note: If you don't happen to have the arrowroot available, you can always use another distinctive tasting spice.

HAROLD'S GRANOLA

This recipe is large so you can make up a big batch, keep it in the refrigerator and eat it in the mornings or whenever you want.

½ cup raisins
½ cup ground almonds or
    walnuts
¼ cup sunflower seeds
½ cup bran flakes
¼ cup corn oil

¼ cup honey
2 cups uncooked oats
½ cup wheat germ
¼ cup ground sesame seed
½ cup shredded coconut
    (unsweetened)
2 tsp. vanilla

Blend the oil, honey, and vanilla together. Mix everything together thoroughly and cook in an oiled baking dish at 300 for 45 minutes. Be careful to mix well every fifteen minutes to prevent burning.

The Battle of Dorm Cooking and some great Sandwiches

The Battle of Dorm Cooking

Mark Archer crept stealthily along the narrow, gloomy hallway. He was a large man, and the small twists and turns in the hallway did little to conceal his bulky frame. Mark had been a Resident Advisor on the third floor for almost two years now. He was a very efficient R.A. who liked his job and took almost sadistic pleasure in catching the violators of various dorm rules and hauling them in to be punished. This particular evening he had heard reports of a young freshman cooking in his dorm room, a direct violation of these rules. As he slid along the shadows, he moistened his lips in anticipation of a fruitful evening. Turning the corner by the drinking fountain, he detected the first wispy scent of cooking vegetables. His heart raced as he quickly glided towards the room at the end of the hall. The blood was pounding in his temples as the slight aroma of cooking vegetables became a wall of asparagus bits and broccoli chunks. As the big R.A. drew next to room 322, he could hear voices barely audible over the blaring stereo. He fumbled with his pass key, the excitement almost overtaking him as he realized he was about to catch not one, but two violators.

Inside, Percy Fussbickle and Henry Blurt heard the clinking of Archer's key chain and they went pale.

A little outrageous? Perhaps, but in many colleges and universities across the country, the case is similar. Suppose you're a freshman at Boony U. You're on room and board and your first day at food service brings an interesting discovery: The food is SO terrible you wouldn't feed it to your dog. After a few weeks, you start losing weight and you begin to wonder how long it will take for you to waste away completely on a diet of ice cream and coffee (two relatively safe cafeteria items). In any event, for various reasons, three weeks into the semester, you go off board and decide to cook in your dorm room.

In some schools, it's perfectly legal to cook in your dorm room. In others, you can get into a lot of trouble if you get caught. This chapter will hopefully give you some ideas on how to survive eating in your room and a few pointers on how not to get caught.

The Arsenal

There are a few types of cooking gear that come in handy when you are trying to whip up something hot and edible in your dorm room. Following is a list of the basic types of cooking equipment available for use in the dorm room; some are obvious, some are not so obvious.

THE CLOTHES IRON

A grilled cheese sandwich can easily be made using an iron as a grill. Just butter the bread, add the cheese, and wrap the whole thing in aluminum foil. Iron. Voila! A perfectly edible grilled (pressed) cheese sandwich. You can also make a skillet out of foil and position it on top of your iron. This skillet can be used to sauté mushrooms or other vegetables.

COFFEE POT

Not just a harmless pot for making coffee, the coffee pot is very versatile when it comes to surviving in your dorm. Naturally, it can be used to heat the water for a Cup-A-Soup or to make instant hot cereal but there's much more. If you just treat a coffee pot as you would a small pot that you use on top of your stove, the possibilities begin to open up. You can use it to boil eggs, to heat up a can of soup, or to cook frozen vegetables, either in a little water or steamed using the kind that come in a pouch. Any "heat up a can and serve" meals cook fine in a coffee pot. If you can get your hands on some leftovers from home or if you know someone with a stove, you can cook up a large casserole and then just reheat it in the coffee pot.

HOT PLATE

Just plug in your hot plate and you've got an instant stove. The thing about hot plates is that you can only fry things at a medium temperature. Foods like bacon that need to be fried at a higher temperature can't be done on a hot plate. If you're living in a dorm that doesn't allow cooking, this item is most probably illegal.

HOT POT

The hot pot is actually a coffee pot adapted for cooking. Where the coffee pot is really not made for anything other than coffee, the hot pot is great for heating water and everything I suggested you cook in your coffee pot. An advantage to using a hot pot over a coffee pot is it's a lot easier to clean. In most dorms, this baby is perfectly legal.

MICROWAVE OVEN

If you can afford one of these, what are you doing in the dorms? I knew one person who had a microwave oven; they are awfully hard to hide if you're not supposed to have them. If you don't know how to cook in one, I suggest you get a hold of a book on microwave cooking as it's a whole science in itself.

THE POPCORN POPPER

What this is made for is popping popcorn. With a stretch of the imagination, it can be used in much the same way as the coffee pot or hot pot, depending on what type you have. Some can be used very efficiently for frying eggs. You can also use it as a fondue pot.

THE STEAM HAIRSETTER

Depending on what kind of hairsetter you can lay your hands on, you can line it with aluminum foil and steam vegetables. Just fold up the edges of the foil so that no butter or cheese or sauce of any type melts into the works. Lay out the vegetables that you want, adding spice, butter and whatever else you would like. Close the top and steam away.

THE TOASTER OVEN

This is probably your best buy in the long run. Spend a few extra dollars and get one that broils and bakes. If you get a good one, it's just like a small oven. You can heat up frozen meat pies and those small frozen pizzas. You can make toast and you can make cookies. You can even broil up a small steak. Actually, the possibilities are endless with these things if you experiment and use your toaster oven to its optimum advantage.

THE ELECTRIC WOK

Although the Chinese have been using woks forever, they have just recently come into their own in the West. You can use a wok for stir frying, steaming and deep frying. The big advantage to having a wok in a dorm room is that it gets very hot and cooks your dinner very fast.

There are a few additional ways that you can cook in your dorm room, but they are not as practical as the others. For example you can use a heating pad to heat up cans of soup or vegetables. You can also make a boy scout stove. You need a short candle, and a one-pound coffee or other can. Just invert the can, and punch some holes in the sides to let the oxygen in and thus keep the flame going. Light the candle and place the can over it. Soon the top of the can will heat up to a suprising temperature that will enable you to fry things. You must be careful where you place it as the candle will drip. Another thing you can do is to wrap your prospective dinner in aluminum foil and somehow fasten it on or near your car engine. Drive somewhere and when you get back you've cooked your dinner (you might have to clear it with the Emission Control Board depending on what you're cooking). You'll have to experiment with that one on your own. That same popcorn popper I mentioned earlier can be used to fry things that don't need too high a temperature. A note here: if you're planning on frying fish or if you're ever cooking anything that emits a rather obvious odor, it's a good idea to do one of several things. First, try not to cook when persons in authority are around. Secondly, if you can't manage to have the authorities absent while you're cooking, at least make an attempt to disguise your doings by stuffing towels under the door and opening your windows wide. When you finish with your illegal activity, spray perfume or deodorizer around to get rid of any lingering food smells. If all this seems like a lot of trouble to go through just to get away with cooking in your room, well, you can always go back to the cafeteria. Or better yet. . .have someone take you out for dinner!

Some Great Sandwiches

One of the principle meals of the dorm-room eater is the sandwich. (When I say "dorm-room eater," I am not referring to someone who eats dorm rooms. . .) If you're like most people, you have probably latched onto a favorite sandwich and then eaten it every day for about two years. Well, variety is important when it comes to food, especially sandwiches. Following are some easy-to-prepare sandwiches that you can eat in your dorm or anywhere else for that matter.

TUNA FISH SANDWICH

There are several different ways to make a tuna fish sandwich, using a variety of ingredients. This one is kind of different from the usual tuna recipe and really tasty. Just mix everything together and spread on the bread. You can add various amounts of mustard, onions, and salt to suit your own tastebuds.

1 8 oz can of tuna fish   3 tbls. relish
1-2 tbls. mayo

CHICKEN SANDWICH

1 tbls. lemon juice   1 cup finely chopped chicken
salt, pepper to taste   ¼ cup finely chopped toasted
pinch of rosemary and thyme   almonds
 (if you have them)   ¼ cup mayo

Mix everything together and spread over bread. Cream cheese is also good on this sandwich.

SALMON SANDWICH

1 7¼ oz. can red sockeye salmon   2 tbls. mayo
2 tbls. chopped onion   ½ tsp. vinegar
3 inch section celery chopped fine

Drain juice from salmon. Combine all ingredients. Spread over any kind of bread, toasted or plain. One can make four sandwiches.

AVOCADO SANDWICH

½ avocado, sliced   lettuce
alfalfa sprouts   tomato
sunflower seeds   mayo

Spread a small bit of mayonnaise on both pieces of bread. Top with a handful of sunflower seeds. Add everything else. I got this recipe from a nifty hole-in-the-wall health food cafe down by the beach. They sell more of these than any other sandwich.

THE HOW-TO-MAKE-BALONEY-TASTE-BETTER SANDWICH

Outside of starving yourself for three days and hiking out of the Grand Canyon to your awaiting piece of baloney, the only way you can make baloney taste better is to disguise the taste. The best way I've found is to use the following ingredients:

Philadelphia cream cheese
alfalfa sprouts
baloney
sliced Monterey jack cheese
sliced tomato

How to Disguise a baloney sandwich

Spread the cream cheese on one side of the bread and add in the rest of the ingredients.

HIGH VITAMIN PROTEIN SANDWICH

½ medium avocado   mayo
small tomato   ¼ cup ground up nuts
½ inch cucumber

Mash the avocado and spread like butter over two slices of bread. Add the ground up nuts, sliced tomato, sliced cucumber, and mayo.

POTATO CHIP SANDWICH

Here's one that sounds crazy but tastes great. Just spread some mayo on one slice of bread, peanut butter on another. Crumble up some potato chips in between and chomp in.

Next are a few sandwiches that need grilling or some other type of cooking. They cannot be made as easily in a dorm room as the above sandwiches but they are just as tasty.

DENVER SANDWICH

1 egg   2 small green onions
1 slice of ham

Beat up one egg with very little milk. Add sliced up green onions (or ordinary onion if you want) and 1 slice of cubed ham. Fry in a small amount of butter. This makes a delicious closed sandwich on toast.

CADILLAC DELIGHT

This is simply a grilled tuna fish sandwich with lettuce and cheddar cheese but it really hits the spot and is a great pick-me-up (the cheese is full of protein).

AVOCADO MELT

½ medium avocado   tomato slice
alfalfa sprouts   jack cheese

Butter one slice of bread as you would to grill. Mash avocado and spread over other side of bread. Add a handful of alfalfa sprouts and tomato slices. Cover with jack cheese and grill 'till cheese melts. Mmmmmmmm!

GRILLED MUSHROOM AND CHEESE SANDWICH

1 piece of fried bacon,   6 slices of fresh mushrooms
  crumbled   cheddar cheese

Sauté mushrooms. Fry bacon crumbled. Place mushrooms and bacon with cheese between the bread; butter and grill.

WEDNESDAY AFTERNOON SPECIAL

beansprouts   Monterey jack cheese
honey wheat bread   slices of tomato

Combine all ingredients on some honey wheat bread and grill.

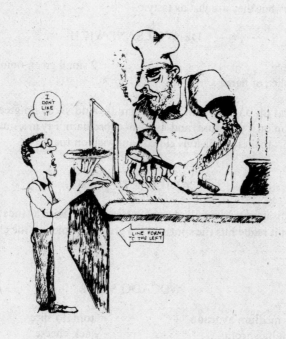

Desserts, Dips, Miscellaneous, etc., and so on...

Desserts, Dips, Miscellaneous, Etc., And So On

Now I know what you're thinking. "Desserts? Dips? What is he rambling on about now? I thought this was a quick and easy recipe book!"

Well, you're absolutely right, this is a quick and easy recipe book and as for my reason for rambling on, I'm not really sure myself. Perhaps it's because I discovered so many good recipes and I couldn't help but want to pass them on. Possibly I wanted to put them in this book all the time so I figured I'd throw desserts and dips in a chapter of their very own along with anything and everything else that didn't fit in any of the other chapters. Maybe I just got carried away in my writing and now nobody in the world can stop me! I'll show them, I'll write forever. Chapters and chapters of the longest cookbook in the world devoted to ridiculously trivial cooking ideas. I can have power, more than I ever dreamed. HA HA HA HA HA HA HA HA HA. They say the radiation from the microwave oven drove me crazy. AHH HA HA HA HA HA HA. . .I say they're the ones that are mad. HE HE HE HE HO HO HA HA.

Desserts

OATMEAL COOKIES

1 cup shortening
1½ cups flour
1½ cups oats (quick rolled type)
1 cup white sugar
½ cup brown sugar

¾ cup chopped walnuts
1½ tsp. vanilla
1 tsp. soda
1 tsp. cinnamon
1 egg

Cream together the white sugar, brown sugar, shortening, and the beaten egg. Set aside. Sift together flour, soda, cinnamon and combine with first mix. Add in everything else and drop by spoon on a greased cookie dish. Butter the bottom of a glass and dip it in sugar. Use the glass to flatten out the cookies as well as coat them with sugar. Bake at 350 for 10 minutes.

CYNDIC'S JELLO

1 large box lime Jello
1 16 oz. small curd cottage cheese

1 8 oz. container Cool Whip
1 8 oz. can crushed pineapple
(strained)

Fold cottage cheese into dry Jello until mixed. Add Cool Whip and strained pineapple. Mix well. Refrigerate for one hour until it sets. Note: Do not make up Jello as directed on the package. Add in dry.

BANANA BREAD

2 cups flour
½ tsp. baking powder
¼ cup butter or margarine
1 cup sugar
½ tsp. baking soda
¼ tsp. salt

1 egg (beaten)
2 large, ripe bananas (use 3 or more for more banana flavor)
3 tbls. sour cream
1 cup chopped walnuts

Combine flour, baking powder, soda, and salt and set aside. Cream butter, add sugar, and work until light and fluffy. Add egg and bananas and mix well. Add flour and sour cream alternately. Add nuts. Pour in a bread pan, bake in 350 (preheated) oven for 40 minutes or until center is done.

SHORT CUT FUDGE

1 can sweetened condensed milk
1 pkg. chocolate chips
1 tsp. vanilla
1 pinch of salt
handful or so of walnuts

Get the water in a double boiler boiling. (If you don't have a double boiler, forget the recipe and just try and say that last sentence 50 times with ice cubes in your mouth.) Place the milk and chocolate chips in the top of the double boiler. Reduce the heat and cook for ten minutes. Add in everything else and place in a pan in the refrigerator for two hours until cool (twenty minutes in the freezer).

Two other quick and easy desserts can be made by scooping out the seeds in half a cantaloupe and filling in the space with a hearty filling of vanilla ice cream. Or, if you're a banana person, you can cut up two bananas in a bowl and sprinkle some sugar over the top. Pour some milk over the whole thing. Great!

Dips

This is the best guacamole dip I, or anybody I know, has ever tasted.

MRS. BRACKER'S GREAT TASTING GUACAMOLE DIP

1 avocado
1 small tomato chopped fine
½ small onion chopped fine
combine above ingredients

add to taste: salt, garlic, pepper
½ lime or lemon juice,
vinegar or oil to give
creamier texture

Mix everything together, taste, and then add a touch of Tabasco sauce if you like it a little hotter.

SHRIMP DIP

4 oz. cream cheese	dash paprika
½ cup Miracle Whip	dash chili powder
½ tsp. garlic powder	1 tsp. dry mustard
½ tsp. onion powder	1 can small shrimp

Cream cream cheese well, add Miracle Whip, blend well. Add everything else. You can add the shrimp in mashed or in bits. Refrigerate, serve.

CALIFORNIA DIP

1 pint sour cream	1 pkg. onion soup mix

Just mix them together and refrigerate before serving.

BEAN DIP

3 cups refried beans	2 tbls. butter
½ tsp. salt	1 cup grated cheddar cheese
1 tsp. garlic powder	¼ cup sour cream
2 tbls. red chili or taco sauce	

Combine all ingredients except sour cream in top of double boiler. Heat just enough to melt the cheese. Stir in the sour cream.

Miscellaneous

Outside of desserts and dips, I also discovered some soup, breakfast, and snack ideas that didn't "blend" well in other chapters.

CLAM CHOWDER

1 7 oz. can minced clams   1 large potato, finely diced
1 medium onion, chopped   2 cups milk
2 slices of chopped bacon   salt and pepper to taste

Fry the bacon and onion together, drain. Add the potato, clam juice, and water enough to cover both. Simmer for 12-15 minutes. Add remaining ingredients, heat and serve when potato is ready.

SPLIT PEA SOUP

1 ham bone (leftover)   4 carrots, finely diced
1 lb. pkg. split green peas   1 celery stalk, finely diced
1 onion finely diced

Combine ingredients in a Dutch oven and completely cover with water. Bring to a boil, reduce heat, and simmer stirring occasionally for 3 hours. Remove the ham bone, pull off the meat and dice it (discarding the fat). Throw the meat back into the pot and cook 1 or 2 more hours. Salt to taste. This is a big recipe so you can always freeze the soup and heat it up later.

BREAKFASTS

Here's a breakfast that will put hair on your chest.

SOME BREAKFAST

1 slice of pineapple (canned)   1 slice of ham
1 banana   2 eggs

Melt some butter in a pan and fry the pineapple. Leave the juice, melt some more butter, peel and slice the banana in half and fry it. Melt some more butter and fry the ham. Add more butter, poach the eggs, and you're set.

ANOTHER GOOD BREAKFAST

Melt plenty of butter in your pan and fry the following:

½ inch slices of mushrooms   ½ inch slices of tomatoes
2 eggs

QUESEDILLAS

Actually, quesedillas are just a Mexican version of a grilled cheese sandwich. A good melting cheese is basic to all quesedillas, but any other addition is up to the individual. You can use flour or corn tortillas, I prefer corn. Just broil in an oven or heat up on a warm pan the open faced tortilla with a small amount of the following ingredients heaped on top:

1 chopped onion	shredded jack and cheddar cheese
sliced olives	1 chopped bell pepper

BROILED BACON AND CHEESE TOAST

1 slice American cheese	1 slice bacon
1 slice bread	

Dice the bacon. Butter the bread and cut it in half. Slice the cheese in half and lay the pieces on the buttered side of the bread. Scatter the diced bacon on top. Place the finished bread on a sheet of aluminum foil on top of a cookie sheet. Place under a broiler until the cheese bubbles, about 3 to 4 minutes. (Watch carefully, they burn easily.) Eat the toast, throw away the aluminimum foil, and don't wash the cookie sheet—it's still clean.

GORP

Just mix together various amounts of the following ingredients:

sunflower seeds (shelled)   dried raisins
peanut M&M's   peanuts
dried coconut   walnuts
granola cereal   dried apricots
almonds

Makes a good snack.

THAT SEAFOOD SAUCE I PROMISED

OK. It's been 15 years since you had fishsticks and you want to see if you still hate them. Or you're the one in 500 people who loves these little monsters. Or you're about to have some other type of seafood, and you've already tried squeezing lemon on them to enhance the flavor. This is a good seafood sauce. Just mix together:

1 cup sour cream   salt, pepper to taste
½ lemon, no skin   ¼ cup ketchup

Etc.

This section is the equivalent of the useful sections you find in other cookbooks. Measurements, terms, the "basic seven," and some really helpful hints. I just hope this isn't the only useful section you have found in this book.

MEASUREMENT EQUIVALENTS

1 lb. - 16 oz.
1 gal. - 4 quarts
1 quart - 2 pints or 4 cups
1 pint - 2 cups
1 cup - 16 tablespoons
1 tablespoon - 3 teaspoons
1 fluid oz. - 2 tablespoons
dash - less than ⅛ teaspoon
pinch - less than ⅛ teaspoon

THE "BASIC SEVEN"

Following is a list of seven types of food. You should try and eat at least one item from each category every day to help provide your body with the minerals and vitamins it needs.

1. Whole grain cereal or bread in some form.
2. Fats: butter, olive oil, etc.
3. Proteins: meat, fish, eggs, cheese.
4. Milk.
5. Citrus fruit, tomatoes, and another fruit; fresh, canned, or frozen.
6. Leafy green or yellow vegetable and another vegetable.
7. One sweet or dessert.

CAPTAIN COOKING'S HELPFUL HINTS

Captain Cooking, as you know, stands for economy, safety, and above all, good taste. He is the protector of freedom and peace in all kitchens throughout the free world (therefore excluding officially communist satellite nations and underdeveloped third world countries where there are no kitchens anyway). Everyday, the Captain battles tasteless and bland dinners, lengthy meal preparations, and dangerous cooking practices that could endanger your life or the lives of your loved ones. But it's a big job and he can't do it alone. The captain would like you, too, to be a defender of these ideals which he holds above all else (or he will feed you to cannibals in South America). To do your share, memorize the words "economy, safety, and good taste" and live by the secret code below:

1. Clean up hint: Use aluminum foil whenever possible to catch drips and limit clean-up task later.

2. If you don't fill all the cups in a muffin tin with batter, put a little water in the empty ones to keep them from burning.

3. Cut onions in running cold water to save your fingers from smelling and your eyes from running.

4. If greens are wilted, run under hot water, then cold, and put in refrigerator until used.

5. Stale bread can be made edible by sprinkling it with a little water and placing in a hot oven for a few minutes.

6. When heating milk, rinse the saucepan first with cold water so that the milk will not form a film on the pan.

7. Clean-up hint: Soak scorched pans or pans used for eggs, doughs, sauces, or puddings in cold water before washing; syrups or fats in hot water.

8. Anything in a can or carton that has been opened keeps better and more flavorful when transferred to glass jars with screw tops.

9. Spaghetti probably won't boil over if you add a tablespoon of cooking oil or butter.

10. Rust can be removed from a sink by using kerosene.

11. Oven fires or fires in pans on the stove caused by grease can be put out right away with salt or baking soda. Never use water.

12. More juice can be obtained from shriveled-up lemons and oranges if you heat them in boiling water for 5 minutes.

13. When baking, results are better if you preheat your pan.

14. Steel wool pads store better in aluminum foil.

15. Place several layers of paper towels on the bottom of your crisper to soak up moisture from washed vegetables and lettuce.

16. Store bread in the refrigerator to prevent molding and make it last longer.

17. Instead of spooning out tomato paste and other impossible substances from a can, just open up the top with a can opener; turn the can over and open the other end. The contents should slip right out.

18. When shopping, always compare packages with the amount you're getting. Larger packages are not always cheaper.

19. The store's own brand of canned goods are usually name brand items re-packaged under the store's name. . .and therefore significantly cheaper.

20. The law states that the ingredients in a package must be listed on the label in order of quantity. Nutritional information is sometimes included also. Read carefully and know exactly what you are and are not paying for.

SOME BASIC TERMS

Although I have assumed in the past that you're capable of handling the terms I've used throughout the book, I still thought it might be a good idea to list some more frequently used cooking terms and their definitions in case you get your hands on some other cookbook (the competition—they're worthless) and it has some unfamiliar words you can't figure out.

BAKE - to cook by dry heat in an oven.
BASTE - to moisten food while cooking, occasionally spooning liquid over meat or other food to prevent it from drying out.
BLANCH - to boil something in water a short time and then immerse it in cold water.
BLEND - to mix two or more ingredients together until they become smooth.
BROWN - to slowly heat something in butter, oil, or water over a medium low temperature, turning occasionally until it is just slightly dark ("browned").

DICE - to chop into small cubes.

DOUBLE BOILER - two saucepans, one fitting on top of the other. The bottom pan holds hot or boiling water so that the contents of the top pan may cook by indirect heat.

ENTREE - the main dish of the meal, usually meat, poultry, or fish.

"FIRE, FIRE" - what you should yell if you notice large black clouds of smoke billowing out of your kitchen.

FOLD - to stir up a mixture by cutting the edge of the spoon through the middle of the mixture and bringing the spoon up by the side of the bowl.

KNEAD - to work dough with the hands, folding over, pressing down, and turning repeatedly.

MARINATE - to tenderize or flavor foods by soaking them in a sauce or other liquid.

MINCE - to chop into very small pieces.

MONOSODIUM GLUTAMATE - a flavor enhancer made from vegetable proteins.

POACH - to cook in hot liquid just below the boiling point.

PREHEAT - to turn the oven on 10-15 minutes ahead of placing the food in so that it's at the proper temperature from the beginning. Always observe this in recipes as it could mean the difference between success and disaster. (Especially with things like cakes and cookies.)

SCALD - to heat up a liquid to just below its boiling point so that a skin forms on top.

SEAR - to brown very quickly.

SIMMER - to cook a liquid just below its boiling point.

SKEWER - long thin pin made of metal or wood used to thread chunks of food.

SOY - an apology spoken by a kindly old Japanese gentleman after he steps on your foot. Also a great flavor enhancer for things like rice, meat, stews, etc.

TOSS - to mix ingredients together loosely.

WHIP - to beat air into a liquid until it becomes thick and frothy.

And So On. . .

Before I finish, I want to add in just two more quick and easy recipes that I just couldn't leave out. These aren't exactly afterthoughts. They're more like after discoveries.

AUNT EDNA'S SWEDISH MEATBALLS

1 lb. ground round
1 bottle chili sauce
1 can cranberries

1 small onion, grated
bread crumbs
1 beaten egg

Mix together the cranberries and the chili sauce, heating the mixture up over a medium temperature for a few minutes. Mix everything else together and roll it up in little balls. Add the little balls into the sauce, sprinkle on a dash of curry, and cook for another half hour covered, basting occasionally.

CHEESE ENCHILADAS

1 can enchilada sauce	1 chopped onion
12 corn tortillas	1 chopped bell pepper
1 lb. grated cheddar cheese	

Fry the tortillas briefly in oil and then dip them in the enchilada sauce. Fill the tortillas with cheese, onion, and peppers, roll them up, and place in a pan. Pour remaining sauce and cheese over the top. Heat up in a 350 oven for about 15 20 minutes or until cheese on top is completely melted. For an extra tasty touch, spoon on some cool sour cream and garnish with a slice of avocado before serving. Note: Two enchiladas per person is usually enough.

Epilogue

Harold (you remember him from the Intro) was happy now. He had learned to cook tasty, quick, and easy meals on a limited budget. No longer did he have to eat beans from a can or heat up frozen T.V. dinners. He found he could eat steak at home cheaper than eating burgers at the local fast food places. With the money he saved in the first year after buying this book, he put himself through real estate school. With the next couple of years' savings, he bought some property at the beach and parlayed his finances into a fortune. Harold not only ate better for less but he won friends, gained influence, and dynamited his sex appeal far beyond his wildest dreams.

As Harold walked into the sunset, past all the fast food chains, he was able to hold his head high knowing that he could cook with economy, safety, and good taste. . .

A Handy Dandy Reorder Form

The Far Out West Publications edition contained the following amusing reorder form.

11 REASONS TO USE THIS HANDY DANDY REORDER FORM

1. This is really a good book, and I would like to give one to my friend.

2. This is really a good book, but I want two for myself.

3. A friend of mine eats like a pig, and I hope this book will straighten him out.

4. It's just about Christmas time, and this book would make a great gift.

5. The paper this book is made from is the only thing my puppy will go to the bathroom on.

6. I have some extra money I was going to throw away anyway.

7. I found this book, and it's got spaghetti all over it. I want a new one.

8. All of the above.

9. This is someone else's book, and I want one of my own.

10. I stole this book and I feel guilty, so I want to have one of my own so I can return this one and have a clear conscience once again.

11. I need another book this exact thickness to help level out my refrigerator.

- -

☐ Please rush me one copy only $4.95
☐ Please rush me one copy only $5.25 I'm a California resident (6% suntan lotion tax) ·
☐ Please rush me_____copies_____each for a total of_____ .
☐ Please rush me 9000 copies at only $4,955.00
☐ Please keep my money and your book.

NAME   Add $1.25 for postage and handling with your
ADDRESS   check or money order to:
CITY   Far Out West Publications
STATE   Box 953
ZIP   South Pasadena, California 91030

(Canadian residents add an additional $1.00)

103